THE
DISCIPLE
~~~
STORY

The Transforming Power
of Scripture

THE
DISCIPLE

STORY

The Transforming Power
of Scripture

Nancy Kruh

Abingdon Press
Nashville

THE DISCIPLE STORY
THE TRANSFORMING POWER OF SCRIPTURE

Cataloging-in-Publication information is available from the Library of Congress

03 04 05 06 07 08 09 10 11 12—10 9 8 7 6 5 4 3 2 1

MANUFACTURED IN THE UNITED STATES OF AMERICA

To my parents,
Robert and Janet Kruh,
who put me on my path to faith
and taught me to be a lifelong learner

CONTENTS

FOREWORD

by Richard B. Wilke

The prophet Amos announced that a day was soon coming when a famine would sweep over the land— a famine not of food or water, but a bloated-belly hunger and a throat-parched thirst for the words of the LORD. When that day comes, shouted Amos, "the beautiful young women and the young men . . . shall fall, and never rise again" (Amos 8:13-14, NRSV).

In recent years, we pastors and other church leaders were slow to see it coming—this life-threatening ignorance of God's Word. We should have spotted it sooner. We should have sniffed the wind and smelled the dryness. Court decisions in our diverse democracy had removed Bible teaching from the public schools. Sunday school attendance had steadily declined since the 1960s. Even in Sunday school, few people brought their Bibles, memory work was out, and the study material got a light touch. In the home—well, most of us were so preoccupied with jobs, school, TV, and an endless stream of activities, that we scarcely had time to eat together as a family, let alone sit by the fireside and read the Bible.

So we were blind-sided, caught off guard even in the 1980s, when we heard reports of graduate students asking, "Who was Jonah?" A Gallup Poll shocked us by reporting that seven out of ten college students could not name the four Gospel writers or more than three of the Ten Commandments. Preaching professors began to write books pleading for narrative sermons built on Bible stories because half the congregation didn't know the background of the message. Perceptive preachers began to realize that they were working amid a desert of Bible ignorance.

In his 1934 drama, *The Rock*, modern prophet T.S. Eliot foretold a society of biblical ignorance and called it a wasteland. "Where My Word is unspoken . . . the wind shall say: 'Here were decent godless people; Their only monument the asphalt road And a thousand lost golf balls.' " As for Amos's prediction that the young women and men would fall down and not get up—I'll let the daily news describe all the social ills that are tearing our world apart.

My wife, Julia, and I woke up to reality while I was pastoring a United Methodist church in Wichita, Kansas, in the late 1970s. We wanted to begin new adult Sunday school classes, but we were having trouble finding lay teachers. Prospects—some long-time church members—said they didn't know enough about the Bible to teach it. We remedied the problem at our church by bringing in a long-term Bible study that had been written in the 1950s, and even with its weaknesses, we saw dramatic changes in the congregation. Faith deepened, new leadership arose, and the church community was strengthened as a whole.

We knew that we had tapped into a hunger, a thirst to know, to read, to actually study the Bible—the same yearning, we soon learned, being murmured by individuals and congregations all across the country. Over time, key leaders began to listen.

In 1986, Julia and I were among a group of ministers,

scholars, educators, and editors who were brought together at a Christian retreat center by The United Methodist Publishing House. We talked about ways to develop a new, intense small-group Bible study in which lives would be transformed. Out of that discussion came a plan to create DISCIPLE Bible Study. Julia and I were privileged to be invited to write the study manual. Our great hope was to reach a small but dedicated band of church leaders around the country. I remember thinking of a specific number— 20,000—that I deemed would make the study an over-whelming success. Little did any of us suspect the whirl-wind of interest that was yet to come.

Since the first of the four phases was released in 1987, DISCIPLE Bible study has been taken more than a million times, and it has exploded into a worldwide movement— translated into several languages, used by more than 30 denominations, inspiring untold numbers to go into the ministry, and transforming countless individual lives.

As Julia and I have traveled the country—and the world—sharing DISCIPLE insights, we've encountered even more delights and surprises. In Virginia, we met a Baptist layman who sold his business, a sports bar, and headed off to seminary. We heard the story in West Virginia of how a study group of older women welcomed a pregnant, unmar-ried teenager, and how, at the study's end, they joined the pastor to help baptize both mother and baby. In Singapore, we sat down with a layman who had volunteered to dub the DISCIPLE videos into Mandarin Chinese so they could be used in mainland China. In Russia, we assisted in a train-ing event with a former TV commentator turned preacher who was leading DISCIPLE in a country where religious prac-tice was once outlawed.

And in too many places to name, we have rejoiced with once-listless congregations now bubbling with spiritual vitality; the pastors explained the difference simply: "DISCIPLE."

Wherever we go, we are humbled to hear the same familiar

words over and over again: "DISCIPLE changed my life." Why has all of this happened? The study's chief editor, Nellie Moser, likes to say it's "a God thing." Julia and I couldn't agree more. Our original enemy was ignorance of the Scriptures, and so we were surprised by the power of the Holy Spirit. We ought not to have been. As Jesus said in Matthew 18:20 (NRSV), "For where two or three are gathered in my name, I am there among them."

Nancy Kruh, veteran feature writer and editor for *The Dallas Morning News*—as well as a DISCIPLE graduate—called on hundreds of study participants over a cup of coffee or on the phone. She gathered story after story behind those words, "DISCIPLE changed my life," and she retells them here in vibrant flesh-and-blood tones. The spiritual journeys are so dramatic, so personal that they make you weep with joy and wonder. As you read *The* DISCIPLE *Story* and share it with others, recall the prophecy of Isaiah 55:11 (NRSV) when God says the word "that goes out from my mouth; it shall not return to me empty, but shall accomplish that which I purpose." And remember the words of our Lord Jesus (John 8:31, The New Jerusalem Bible) that have become the credo of Disciple, "If you make my word your home you will indeed be my disciples."

ACKNOWLEDGMENTS

Over the course of many months, I approached scores of DISCIPLE Bible Study participants around the country, asking if they would share their stories for this book. Not a single person turned down my request, and perhaps that—as much as anything—testifies to the power of this study. DISCIPLE graduates not only are comfortable talking openly and candidly about their faith, but they also welcome the opportunity, even to a stranger with a thousand questions. For me, that was one of two great blessings that came from working on this book. The other was the immense impact all of these remarkable witnesses have had on my own faith and my personal understanding of the Bible.

My greatest regret is not being able to include the stories of everyone who shared with such generous spirit. To these people, I can only offer my heartfelt gratitude, as well as assurances that while their accounts may not appear on these pages, every story I gathered has influenced the writing of this book. Among this number I wish to thank in particular are Jim Texter, Jim Cates, Kevin and Terry Meade, Todd Bristow, Jo-Ann Nitta Bristow, Laurie Hynson, Mary Krisely, Jo Lynch, Joy Perry, Annelda Crawford and her DISCIPLE class, Dominique Johnson, Gail Nelson, and Ken and Iweeta McIntosh.

Many of the DISCIPLE graduates featured in this book selflessly shared with me some of their most private thoughts and painful moments solely out of a desire to inspire others to Bible study. Everyone I spoke to placed enormous trust in me to tell their stories, and I hope this work shows that I have earned it. Among those I want to especially thank are Steve and Sue Gill and their DISCIPLE class, Barry Trantham, Lynda Rhodes, Todd and Marti Martin, Steve Tucker, Becky Scrivner, Susan Hellums, Rev. Zan Holmes, Jr., Rev. Mike Cave, Rev. Beryl Notman, Rev. Jim Chaplain, Kelvin Smith, and Claudia Lovelace.

Many more people—pastors, church personnel, and DISCIPLE leaders—eagerly assisted me in tracking down the sources for the stories on these pages. Among those I wish to thank are Bishop Ernest Lyght, Evelyn R. Brunson, Rev. Stan Basler, Jim Coy, Martha Flavell, Rev. April Bristow, Liz Davis, Rev. Bob Ward, Rev. Tom Tate, Judy Owsley, Rev. Clark Hess, Betty Piper, Ed Allred, and Wini Grizzle and her staff at The United Methodist Publishing House.

I also wish to offer my gratitude to Tait Berge for allowing me to use excerpts of his copyrighted autobiography, *My Exodus*; Rev. Bill Power, professor emeritus at Perkins School of Theology at Southern Methodist University, and Dr. Leander Keck, professor emeritus at Yale Divinity School, for their keen insight into the subject of Bible study; and Dr. David Roozen, director of the Hartford Institute for Religion Research at Hartford Seminary, for his expertise on trends in Bible study.

Many staff members at The United Methodist Publishing House have worked with great diligence to make this book a reality. I am particularly grateful for the care and commitment of Harriett Olson, Judy Smith, Mark Price, Katherine Bailey, Michael Russell, and Linda Spicer.

I save my final thanks for the four principals who breathed life into DISCIPLE and turned it into such a dynamic force in the fields of Bible study, faith growth, and personal transformation. I offer my most sincere gratitude to Nellie Moser and Wini Grizzle for the recollections they shared with such passion and insight; I'm appreciative, as well, for all the enthusiasm they have shown for this book. Most of all, I wish to express my profound gratitude to Dick and Julia Wilke, who coaxed and encouraged me into this project and have been my guiding lights and my muses throughout. I'm also grateful for the support of every member of the Wilke family, especially Sarah Wilke, who offered me constant inspiration, unflagging encouragement, gentle criticism, and rare wisdom from the moment I decided to undertake this book. I could not have done it without her.

FROM DARKNESS
INTO LIGHT

The whole group had been looking forward to this day for what seemed an eternity. Finally, after a year's break, the twelve men and women, all residents of suburban New York, would be coming back together for another long-term Bible study. Of course, they had seen one another frequently during that year—at Sunday worship, at holiday get-togethers and other social events. They'd talked often by phone. But still, it hadn't been the same.

Now they were once again ready to commit themselves to the daily reading and the weekly meetings. Tonight they would all gather again at Steve and Sue Gill's warm and roomy two-story home, the same place they'd always met before. Tonight would be the orientation for INTO THE WORD INTO THE WORLD, another in the four-part DISCIPLE Bible study series.

Steve Gill would be arriving by train from the city, where

he worked at the World Trade Center. Diane Kenney Lewis would be coming from her job at a nearby college; John Talbot from his literary-agency office in his apartment; Debbie Slansky from her video-editing table at her home; Grace Powers from her high school art studio.

It was going to be a day of hopeful new beginnings, if all went as planned. But nothing went as planned the day of September 11, 2001.

The Unimaginable News

"Terrors overwhelm me," the author of the book of Job wrote, ". . . [and] my safety vanishes like a cloud" (30:15, NIV). These Old Testament words were written thousands of years ago, yet they could have spoken for everyone in New York City at 8:47 that morning—the moment a band of terrorists turned a jetliner into a bomb and smashed it into the north tower of the World Trade Center.

At that moment, Steve Gill was having a business breakfast in a hotel restaurant located at the base of the south tower. Everyone in the room heard what sounded like an explosion. The restaurant was transparent—the walls and roof were made of glass—and all eyes turned upward. What they saw was a cascade of glass and debris about to crash down on them.

At that same moment, Sue Gill was at home with a plumber who was putting in a new toilet. The phone rang. It was the Gills' oldest son, calling from his office in Connecticut. He'd just received an e-mail from a friend: "You're not going to believe this, but the World Trade Center is on fire." Sue ran to turn on the television; and as she stood and watched in utter disbelief, a second plane plunged into the south tower. In those first jumbled minutes of shock, she didn't allow herself to think the unthinkable—that her husband might be in harm's way. After all, the planes had hit the 110-story Twin Towers; his office was on the twenty-seventh floor of World Trade Center 7, a much smaller structure across the street. Then another call came, this time from Steve's secretary. She was still at her home in New Jersey, and she was hysterical. She knew Steve had had the breakfast meeting, and she knew where it was. She wanted to know: Had Sue heard from him? Sue's heart froze. Suddenly, she didn't know if her husband of thirty years was dead or alive.

One by one that morning, the Gills' DISCIPLE classmates heard the unimaginable news of what was occurring just a few miles away. And as horror piled upon horror, their thoughts turned to Steve Gill. He hadn't been one of the group's two co-leaders, but over the course of the thirty-four-week Bible study, he had become their anchor. The fifty-two-year-old international banker could seem so reserved and businesslike with his tailored suits and precise British accent. But the Steve Gill everyone in the group knew was also the one who could crack everybody up with an unexpected wry comment. He was the guy who could rock out with his electric guitar in the Circuit Riders, the Christian band that several members of the church had formed. He also was the one with the most well-worn Bible; the margins were covered with scribbled notes, and passages had been highlighted and rehighlighted. More often than not, Steve's comments moved the group's discussions to a deeper perspective.

Now all of his classmates were caught in a balance between hope and fear. What was the fate of this man they had come to cherish? In those first desperate hours, there was a flurry of phone calls among the group's members—to talk to Sue, to talk to one another. Those who could, rushed to the Gills' home to sit and wait. Wherever they were, all of them, in their own way, stopped to do what they had done together during the thirty-four-week Bible study. They prayed.

Transformation, Inside and Out

By that day, every one of these dozen people believed they had come into one another's lives because God had brought them together. It certainly hadn't started out that way. Like most of the hundreds of thousands of people who have enrolled in a DISCIPLE class since its introduction in 1987, these twelve did so for one simple reason: They wanted to know more about the Bible.

Indeed, this most holy book of the Christian faith is a spiritual and literary masterpiece, but it also can be overwhelming. The typical Bible runs two thousand pages, and it's filled with unfamiliar language, strange characters, fantastic stories, and a God of staggering complexity. Most biblical experts agree that even to begin to grasp the contents in their entirety requires time, discipline, and guidance.

But as the dozen New Yorkers had found, the people drawn into DISCIPLE often get far more than the Bible knowledge they yearned for. The introductory handbook that describes the first study in the series, BECOMING DISCIPLES THROUGH BIBLE STUDY, hints at the possibilities. "The hoped-for results," it says, are "biblically nourished persons committed to live as disciples." But the handbook can't begin to tell the story—lived out thousands of times—of how people can struggle over the Scripture and somehow be transformed, both individually and collectively.

The transformation may be inward; many who have completed a DISCIPLE Bible study come to experience a richer and more intimate relationship with God. Or the transformation may be outward. For some, it can be as simple and straightforward as becoming more generous with their time, money, and talents. For others, it can be profound. The DISCIPLE experience has inspired marriages to be mended, career paths to be redrawn, even entire lives to be rebuilt.

Transformation can also occur in the group itself. The

earliest Christian congregations didn't sit in church pews and listen to a preacher's sermon. The New Testament describes them gathering in private homes, building bonds with one another as they discussed scriptural teachings. So it is with DISCIPLE groups. What begins as a roomful of acquaintances, or even strangers, often ends as a community tightly joined by love and Christian devotion.

To realize any of these transformations, though, has always required a leap of faith. When the new pastor at Steve and Sue Gill's church, First United Methodist of Mamaroneck, New York, announced the formation of DISCIPLE classes in 1999, the level of commitment gave everyone pause. The church had had other Bible studies in the past, but these had lasted only a few weeks and dwelled mostly on the New Testament. The foundational DISCIPLE study—the one that offers a grand sweep of the Bible—requires participants to read more than 70 percent of the Scripture. At least one person in the group would have to undergo three days of training to be a leader. Then, for nine months, the class members would have to spend three to four hours a week in individual study and come together weekly for a two-and-a-half-hour group experience. The gathering wouldn't be driven by lectures; everyone would be required to participate in discussion.

"I didn't know if I would be able to do it," says John Talbot, a literary agent in his late thirties who lives in Mamaroneck, about a dozen miles north of Manhattan. "It seemed like a huge commitment." Still, he was attracted to the study by what he thought was "an intellectual approach" to the Bible. Besides that, since he and his wife had joined the church three years before, they had become good friends of the Gills, and Sue had agreed to co-lead a class.

Both the Gills had grown up in the church in England. High school sweethearts, they married in their early twenties and had two sons, and Steve built a successful career in banking. The family had lived in the New York area, off and on, since 1987. Like her husband, Sue Gill had been a lifelong student of the Scripture. In fact, she had read and reread it so many times she felt she had wrung everything out of it that she could. She hoped DISCIPLE would change that.

Two classes were formed at the church that year, divided not by existing friendships but by which weeknight was most convenient for each participant. The Gills' group of fifteen would meet on Tuesday evenings. It was a varied assortment of friends and casual acquaintances; some recognized each other only by face. They were all different ages (from their twenties to their fifties), income levels, and occupations. A few, like the Gills, felt at home in the Scripture; others were barely familiar with the stories of Jesus. In fact, about the only thing they all had in common was the small steepled church they attended.

Debbie Slansky, a forty-nine-year-old videographer, was talked into taking the study by the church's associate pastor, Chuck Van Houten, the group's other co-leader. The mother of four had recently returned to church after a life of hard knocks that had even included a stretch of homelessness. "It was kind of surreal that I would even show up at a Bible study," says Debbie, who had always considered herself "a loner."

The DISCIPLE study manual determined the five Scripture readings for the week, and these generally followed the same order as the Bible. The reading for the sixth day was the manual itself—commentary offering background and context to the Bible passages, as well as questions designed to help participants grapple with the Scripture.

The group met on the seventh day of the study week to discuss what they had read. Initially, the conversations were hesitant. Several members had never had an opportunity for such open deliberation over matters of faith. Steve Gill quickly took on the role of icebreaker, says Chuck Van

Houten. "Here was someone who knew a lot about the Bible, but he still could learn, and he was willing to say that," says the associate pastor. "That validated the other people, and sort of gave them permission to feel it was O.K. to be a novice."

Week by week, the inhibitions began to fade. "At first, I thought I'd be quiet," says Debbie Slansky. "But the more I learned, the more I wanted to know, and I wanted to talk about it and debate."

Whatever the lesson, the class learned to apply three questions that are crucial to understanding the Bible: What does this passage say about God? What does this say about people? What does this say about the relationship between God and people?

Often, the responses were no less than revelations, says Chuck Van Houten. "Not to make it sound too grandiose," he says, "but you could really see people come to realizations. I think that's what makes the Bible the 'living word.' The Spirit works today, just as it did on the day the Scripture was being written."

Diane Kenney Lewis had a revelation as the study moved through the Old Testament. Before taking DISCIPLE, she considered the Bible's earliest writings to be a litany of carnage and retribution. She had never been able to reconcile what she considered the Old Testament God of vengeance with the New Testament God of love. But now, she was absorbing something totally different. "I saw God always reaching out to his children, very much like a parent," says the program secretary, who works at the College of New Rochelle nearby. "Here was God trying to make these covenants, and no matter how much he tried, people kept messing up. But he kept trying. God wants to be with us. God wants a relationship with us."

John Talbot made his own stunning discovery. He actually saw his own reflection in these odd, ancient biblical characters. On page after page, here were all the familiar traits—love and hate, hope and despair, joy and suffering. Yes, the world had progressed, but the human experience had stubbornly stayed the same. "I think that's what a lot of us didn't anticipate—to correlate what's going on in the Bible with what's going on today," he says. "There's a great comfort in knowing that people were just the same back then, and that there's a way to address it."

Once the connections were made, it seemed only natural for the group to begin talking about themselves. "People shared with one another in the light of all we were learning in God's Word," says Chuck Van Houten. "I think they began to see God putting them into each other's lives."

An unusual number of stresses and turning points were being experienced among this group of fifteen that year. Marriages were beginning and ending; family members were sick or even dying; careers were in upheaval. A shared confidence not only evoked empathy from other group members; it also began weaving connections. Often, the most intimate time came at the end of class when the group held hands in a circle and took turns praying aloud.

Somehow, the lessons and classes seemed to come along at just the right time in their lives. The group met, for instance, on the day Sue Gill got word her mother had suffered a serious heart attack in London. "I had DISCIPLE," she recalls, "and I stood there, hand in hand, and they all prayed for me. Then I flew out." As her mother lay dying, she continued to receive comfort and support from classmates by telephone.

At first, Grace Powers found the closeness of the group a little unsettling. "I never had that before—being able to open up and share problems," says the sculptor and high school art teacher. But even though she warmed to the opportunity of reaching out to her classmates, it wasn't until the last days of the study that she found the courage to tell them of her own private pain: She was in the midst of a divorce. The comfort she had given through the months was instantly returned as the group laid hands on her and offered prayers.

After the study was completed, the group's initial impulse was to jump immediately into another one of the four parts in the series. But they resisted. For nine months, they had tightened, like the fingers of two hands folded in prayer. Now it was time to open those hands and extend them. It was time to be disciples.

Over the next year, they committed themselves to new church activities, joining committees or the choir. They also undertook quiet ministry, simply seeing a need—a hospital visit, a homecooked meal—and filling it. Steve Gill and his Christian rock band continued playing concerts around the area and at the monthly contemporary service at the church. John Talbot took a leading role in a men's prayer group. Debbie Slansky began exploring a call to the ministry.

Still, the plan had always been to come back together eventually, and in the summer of 2001, a dozen from the original group signed up for another phase of the study series that was scheduled to start on September 11.

The Tense Calm Is Broken

That morning, Debbie Slansky sat on the edge of her bed and watched on television as the second plane slammed into the World Trade Center's south tower. "My God, my God, my God." Her lips endlessly mouthed the words; there was nothing else to say. She pulled on a pair of pants and rushed over to the Gills' home.

When she got there, she found the downstairs filled with familiar faces. The Gills' two sons and daughter-in-law were there; so were other members of the DISCIPLE group and friends from church. Sue had just spoken to a stranger who had called from his cell phone. "Your husband," he said, "is O.K. and in a safe place." Then he hung up.

This tiny shred of information delivered the news that Steve Gill was alive, but it also brought all new anxieties. Why wasn't he the one calling? Where was he? Was he hurt? The waiting and praying continued.

The telephone calls kept coming, all from friends wanting to know if there had been any word. No, nothing yet. Then around eleven o'clock—more than two hours since the attack began—the telephone rang again. Sue picked it up and heard all that she'd been longing to hear: her husband's voice. Steve was all right. He was calling from the Staten Island Ferry. The tense calm in the room gave way to sobs of relief. "It was like a flood," recalls Debbie Slansky.

Steve had borrowed the cell phone of a coworker he'd run into on the ferry; it was the first opportunity he'd had to call. He told his family he loved them and that he would be home as soon as he could.

Around seven o'clock that evening, the barks of the Gills' shepherd, Jo Jo, announced his arrival. As soon as Steve Gill walked through the door, his dark hair still covered in dust, he was enveloped by family and friends. Soon, someone suggested a prayer in gratitude for his safe return. They prayed too for those still waiting for loved ones to come home—and for those whose loved ones never would.

Shock, Grief, and Fear

For the members of the DISCIPLE group, the days that followed were consumed by the horror that had arrived at the doorstep of their suburban community. For that matter, the whole New York area was running on raw emotion. With untold numbers missing or dead and thousands more escaping from the site, everyone seemed to know someone directly affected by the tragedy—a relative, a neighbor, a coworker, a friend, or a friend of a friend.

The attack had managed to invade every sense. For miles around, the stench of electrical fire hung heavily in the air.

Newspapers and television brimmed with reports. Conversation turned to nothing else. Any distant rumbling evoked sudden panic: Was it thunder? a fighter jet scanning the skies? or another hijacked airplane? Most people found it difficult to do even the simplest tasks.

With his workplace destroyed by the falling towers, Steve Gill set about to help manage the bank's multibillion-dollar business from his home, then from a rented conference room at a nearby hotel. But this consummate professional, who'd always seemed so unflappable, also was hardly eating and was sleeping fitfully. Tears came often and uncontrollably. Struggling with her own swirl of feelings, Sue Gill tried to reach out, but her husband kept her at arm's length. Others in the DISCIPLE group wheeled between shock, grief, and fear. Grace Powers spent listless hours on her couch. Debbie Slansky couldn't go a day without crying.

Despite the extraordinary circumstances, the group decided to postpone the start of the study, INTO THE WORD INTO THE WORLD, only a week. Everyone came, though mostly because they just wanted to be together. It was no use trying to do anything but go through the motions of orientation. "Everyone had that sheen of stress sweat," recalls John Talbot.

Once they began their daily Bible readings, they all found they had trouble concentrating. "I'm so sad and angry that I can hardly breathe," Debbie Slansky wrote down in the first lesson of her study manual. During class, co-leaders Sue Gill and Diane Kenney Lewis (who had replaced Chuck Van Houten after he was transferred to another church) found it difficult to keep the discussion on the readings. "It started out on the Scripture," says Sue Gill, "then it led into September 11. People really had to talk about it."

During one of the early classes, someone mustered the courage to ask Steve Gill exactly what had happened to him that morning. In a manner both subdued and direct, he recounted his story. He told how he and the other restaurant patrons had managed to lunge out of the way as the debris came crashing through the roof. Then how everyone in the room was led out onto the street, where they faced even more showers of glass and debris. The north tower's gaping wound wasn't visible from where they stood, so no one knew exactly what was happening. Somehow, Steve and his four breakfast companions managed to run the gauntlet. Then, just as they had gotten away, something caught Steve's ear. He looked up at the moment the second jetliner crashed into the south tower.

The mood on the street turned from urgency to panic. Everyone began to scatter in different directions. Steve and his four companions headed south toward the bay shore. About four blocks away, they stopped to rest, thinking they were out of danger. Steve spotted a stranger with a cell phone and asked him to get a message to Sue. As the five lingered, there was a sudden rumble. Steve turned around. What he saw was beyond imagining. The south tower was collapsing, melting as if it were a candle. Now the five were running; but within moments, the billowing clouds of ash and dust overtook them, plunging them into a choking darkness. Covering their faces with cloth, Steve and his four companions clung to one another as they blindly inched their way south. The sound of the second tower's collapse was so indistinct and the air was already so black, Steve told his DISCIPLE classmates, he didn't even know it was occurring.

By the time the five got near the water's edge, the dust had cleared enough for them to see their way to the Staten Island Ferry terminal. Once inside, they brushed themselves off as best they could and waited for a ferry. All the telephone lines were down, but once aboard the ferry, Steve ran into the coworker with a cell phone and finally made his call home.

The group listened in hushed silence as Steve finished the story. Then Debbie Slansky asked him a question. "When did you finally feel safe?"

"I'll let you know when it happens," he answered.

The Timelessness of Scripture

During the first Bible study the year before, the group had drawn tight helping one another cope with personal anguishes. Now, the group was confronting a communal pain. While Steve Gill was the only one who had actually been at ground zero, every member in his or her own way felt adrift after September 11. But gradually, almost instinctively, they began feeling their way back to the familiar ground of Scriptures.

In only the second week of readings, the class received a jolting reminder of the Bible's timelessness. The assignment featured the story of the Tower of Babel—a structure built to reach the heavens that instead came crashing down. Grace Powers could hardly believe the similarities. "This is too weird," she wrote in her study manual.

While this study dealt with Genesis and Exodus more thoroughly than the original one, the class members were still reading familiar stories—of Adam and Eve, Noah and the ark, Abraham and the rest of the patriarchs. This time around, though, the writing seemed to wield an even greater power. "To me, it had more relevancy and more urgency," says John Talbot.

The scale of the September 11 tragedy was moving the group into issues that had seemed almost academic before: Is there really such a thing as evil? Where do you draw the line between seeking justice and seeking revenge? And perhaps most pressing of all, if God is all powerful, then why did something so terrible occur?

On the latter question, there was vigorous discussion but no real conclusion. "I don't think God does these things," says Diane Kenney Lewis, but she doesn't know why. "I think, in a way, humans are infants compared to God. You aren't meant to understand."

Steve Gill reflected on the suffering that God's own son, Jesus Christ, had to endure on the cross. "Part of the Christian life is dealing with the reality of evil and sin, and choosing what you are going to do," he says. "And walking in faith is one of the key responses."

Before September 11, John Talbot had tended to see life's complexities in shades of gray; but the attacks left him with no doubt about the darkness of evil. "I really believe that evil is caused by human beings who are disconnected from God," he says, "and there is a constant struggle between good and evil."

One evening Steve Gill brought to class a psalm he'd run across. He'd heard it referred to as the "terrorist psalm":

> "Hide me from the secret plots of the wicked,
>> from the scheming of evildoers. . . .
> They hold fast to their evil purpose;
>> they talk of laying snares secretly,
> thinking, 'Who can see us?
>> Who can search out our crimes?
> We have thought out a cunningly conceived plot.'. . .
> But God will shoot his arrow at them;
>> they will be wounded suddenly.
> Because of their tongue he will bring them to ruin;
>> all who see them will wag their heads"
>
> (Psalm 64:2-8, RSV).

The passage helped the group cope with their anger. "I think part of being a Christian," says Steve, "is standing strong against evil, and that means stopping the hand that's bringing down the sword. But we've seen in history that evil collapses on its own weight, and God exercises justice on it."

One by one the class members were finding personal ways to respond to the new world around them. Grace Powers saved news photos and painstakingly assembled two collages for the covers of her DISCIPLE study manual—the Twin Towers' destruction on the back, the recovery on the front. "I couldn't focus for a month," she says. "It helped me reground myself." Debbie Slansky put together a photo album of the rescue and recovery efforts, inscribing each photo with a Scripture, and gave it to Steve Gill. "He was gracious, as usual," she says, "but it was probably therapy more for me."

Someone in the group suggested everyone pocket what they would spend for lunch once a week and put the cash in a pool. By the spring of 2002 the fund had reached several hundred dollars, and the members began talking about how to use it. The consensus was not just to give it away but to find a way to be part of a ministry. John Talbot already was considering how to make his own new commitment to the community. "In DISCIPLE," he says, "the question every week is, how do you bring your faith out into the world?"

Steve Gill was perhaps the one dealing with the biggest life changes of all. He had been thinking about leaving his job even before September 11, but the experiences of that day pushed him to a crossroads. As he read in Genesis 12 how God called Abraham to leave behind all he'd ever known, Steve saw—as he never had seen before—how difficult it must have been to respond. Yet Abraham picked up and went, not even knowing where God was leading him.

"I feel a bit like Abraham when God says, your old order is gone, now go," Steve says. "I say, 'O.K., what do you mean?'" But Abraham, Steve realized, didn't stop to ask questions. "It was a faith based on responding to what God said, not on having all the answers."

As Sue Gill reconnected with her husband, she saw how he was working more than ever to put himself in God's hands. In early 2002, he finally made a decision. He left the bank and launched a new consulting business designed to help corporations cope with change and crisis. As with everything else in his life, his Christian faith is at its center. "I haven't the first idea what will happen," he says, "but I'm excited to find out what God's got in store."

During the first Bible study, Pastor Chuck Van Houten said something one night that stuck with the group: "God does not will bad things to happen, but he will make good out of bad." Of course, at the time, no one could have imagined how those words would be put to the test on September 11, 2001.

But since that day of devastation, the twelve members of this DISCIPLE Bible study class had come together to be transformed. As they journeyed through the Scripture, they had found comfort and healing, strength and understanding, a new sense of purpose, and a deepening faith.

No one ever doubted that these were all gifts from God.

CHAPTER TWO

FEEDING THE HUNGER

W hen DISCIPLE Bible study was introduced in 1987, no one involved in its creation expected or even anticipated the magnitude of its impact.

Because of public response, what was supposed to be just one study eventually evolved into a series of four studies. Cumulatively, by 2001, the four had passed the million mark for enrollment. DISCIPLE has reached into all fifty states and has been translated into several languages for thousands who've taken it around the world. More than twenty thousand people from many Christian denominations have taken the training to be study leaders. DISCIPLE has become the backbone of congregations, the source of an untold number of calls to ordained ministry, and—perhaps most significantly—the catalyst for meaningful change in hundreds of thousands of lives.

How this Bible study came to be—and came to be all that it is—is a story that begins at what DISCIPLE editor Nellie Moser likes to call a "kairos moment." The word is Greek, the original language of the New Testament, and it means "the right time." To Moser, as well as the other principals in the project, DISCIPLE spun out of the perfect synchronicity of people, ideas, need, and opportunity. As far as she and the others are concerned, the timing had nothing to do with luck. "This study was given to us by God. I believe that," says Moser.

A Decline in Bible Literacy

By the early 1980s, Moser's employer, The United Methodist Publishing House in Nashville, Tennessee, had identified a need nationally for more Bible study. At the time, several studies—created by a variety of sources—were already in existence. Most were only a few weeks in length and were led by trained lecturers; the United Methodist contribution was in the form of Sunday school curriculum. Still, surveys clearly showed the public hungered for more, according to Tom Potter, who directed the publisher's market research at the time. But what exactly would feed that hunger, he says, was a wide-open question. Though commitment was in place to develop some sort of study, say Potter and other key figures, the publishing house struggled to find a starting place.

Around that same time, about 750 miles away, a United Methodist minister was discovering in his own church how an intense, long-term Bible study could revitalize a congregation. When Richard B. Wilke and his wife, Julia, arrived at First United Methodist Church in downtown Wichita, Kansas, in 1974, it was a church in decline. Though the congregation had about twenty-five hundred members, making it the largest the Wilkes had ever served, that number was still a thousand less than what it had been in recent years. As these two lifelong partners in ministry worked to diagnose the cause of the decrease, they realized that the church's most resilient element was its dozen or so adult Sunday school classes, even though a new one hadn't been formed in fifteen years. The loyalty was astonishing. Each week, almost without fail, class members made the trek from the suburbs for the fellowship and a smattering of Bible-based study. Forming new classes, the Wilkes decided, would be crucial to reigniting the church. But whom could they recruit to teach?

The first member Wilke approached was an attorney, a third-generation member who was a regular in the pews. To Wilke's surprise, the man turned him down flat. "I don't know enough Scripture," he confessed to his new pastor. "I would be embarrassed to stand up in front of adults and talk about the Bible."

The response shook Wilke to his toes. One reason new classes had never formed, he quickly deduced, was because so few people felt qualified to teach them. He began to put the pieces together. During his two decades in Kansas pulpits, he had witnessed a slow, steady decline in Bible literacy among his congregations. But he'd never reflected deeply on the damage that decline was doing to the church.

Throughout their own lives, the Wilkes had taken their love of Scripture almost for granted. Wilke grew up in the 1930s and 1940s above his family's funeral home in Eldorado, Kansas, and the recitation of Bible passages served as almost a soundtrack to his childhood. As a child in Texarkana, Texas, Julia Wilke eagerly signed up for a twelve-week course that required her to memorize 240 Bible verses; her reward, a plaque of praying hands, is still proudly displayed in her home. During both of their childhoods, hearing and reading Scripture were common occurrences at church, in Sunday school, at church camp, even in public school.

But three decades later, their background appeared no longer the norm. Plainly, this missing element was sapping the strength of their church. Christians whose faith wasn't based on the Bible's teachings, the Wilkes sensed, didn't fully understand God's claim on their lives. The result was a weakening—both in people's relationship with God and in the ties within the Christian community. The key to building new leadership and reviving the church, the Wilkes concluded, was a long-term, comprehensive Bible study.

The couple set out on a search for a suitable product, each bringing to the mission separate but complementary abilities. As a pastor and accomplished pulpit preacher, Richard Wilke had keen insight into the issues of congregational growth and communication. As a former public school teacher and seasoned Sunday school instructor, Julia Wilke possessed expertise in education and lay development.

Eventually, they settled on a Bible study that had been introduced in 1959 by a Lutheran minister. Wilke and an associate pastor underwent ten days of teacher training. Then, for the next two years, they led a weekly class of about fifteen church members, including Julia Wilke, to turn them into Bible lecturers. Once this new platoon of instructors was trained, students were recruited from the congregation. This was no Sunday school social hour; most classes were scheduled on weeknights and lasted two-and-a-half hours. Yet the congregation flocked to enroll, and out of these classes a whole new generation of lay leaders emerged. The church began its turnaround, and the Wilkes knew they had stumbled onto something powerful. They weren't sure at all, though, how they could take their discovery any farther than their own church.

Then, in 1984, Wilke was elected a United Methodist bishop and appointed to oversee the churches of Arkansas. Now with a voice in national church leadership, he began to use it with force. Why, he wanted to know, had the church lost a million members in the previous decade, and what could be done about it? His outspokenness soon caught the ears of upper management at The United Methodist Publishing House, and he was invited to write a book. The result, entitled *And Are We Yet Alive?*, was released in 1986 and rapidly found critical success. It was both a terse diagnosis of what ailed the church and a lively prescription for its recovery; among the recommendations was long-term Bible study.

The denomination, Wilke argued, was paying the price for the decline in Bible literacy. It was time to change that. "The Bible is our book," he wrote, "and we will carry it into the future with us. We will teach it to our people, and they will in turn teach it to others. Pastors must multiply themselves by training others." After naming Bible studies already available, he urged: "Other plans for training lay teacher/disciplers need to be prepared quickly."

He had no way of knowing that, within a year, he and his wife would be writing one of those "other plans."

Blueprint for a Bible Study

In early 1986, Jim Beal, a Methodist pastor in Arkansas, called publishing house editor Nellie Moser with a question; the two had become acquainted while serving on a denominational committee. Trying to reproduce his success in Wichita, Richard Wilke, Beal's bishop, had recently issued a directive for every United Methodist minister in the state to teach a comprehensive Bible study at their churches. Why, Beal asked, wasn't there a United Methodist product that fit the bill?

Moser thought it was a question worth pursuing, even though it didn't directly involve her responsibilities as executive editor of youth and adult curriculum. Still, she had a keen interest in the Bible. In fact, her passion for biblical history had taken her numerous times to Israel for archaeological digs. She told Beal she'd bring up the issue with Claude Young, the vice-president of the book-publishing division.

Within days, Wilke found himself chatting by telephone

with Young. Because of Wilke's newly released book, the two men didn't need any introductions. Young explained that the publishing house was looking for new ideas for a Bible study. The two launched into a lively dialogue about Wilke's experiences and those of his wife. Soon it was agreed that the couple would come to Nashville and present their recommendations. The surprise invitation was an opportunity of a lifetime for the Wilkes. They would be able to reflect on their own insights—into what was effective as well as on what fell short—and try to build a better Bible study.

Around a large conference table at the Nashville headquarters, a group of executives and editors gathered to hear the Wilkes' presentation; among them were Moser and publishing house president Robert Feaster. Several in the room had never met the couple, but the husband and wife made an immediate impression. At six feet two inches tall, Wilke has a commanding presence; his five-foot-nine-inch-tall wife also seems somewhat larger than life. He exudes an almost electric energy; she balances him with a sunny warmth.

Wilke took center stage, mapping out about two dozen characteristics the couple believed would create an ideal platform for learning about the Bible. They wanted, among other things, a study that would

- cover the Bible from start to finish, with equal emphasis on the Old and New Testaments. The Wilkes felt this would allow students to grasp the "unfolding drama of salvation history"; it also would set the study apart from Sunday school curriculum, which tended to offer the Scripture in bits and pieces.

- allow the Bible to speak for itself. A study manual would offer history and context, rather than theological interpretation, making it accessible to a wide range of believers.

- require substantial daily reading and weekly group meetings. This would allow students to encounter Scripture on their own as well as to create a habit of Bible reading. Also, the Wilkes had witnessed for themselves how weekly meetings for discussion, sharing, and prayer could turn a group into a small but dynamic community of faith.

- accommodate groups of about twelve. As the number of Jesus' disciples, twelve had powerful Christian symbolism. Besides that, on a more practical level, most living rooms can accommodate about that many people, and the Wilkes' preference was for classes to be held in the comfortable surroundings of home, rather than around a church meeting table.

- have a leader, not a lecturer. This so-called "learner among learners" would simply direct the flow of discussion. This arrangement would stimulate group discussion and eliminate the need for extensive teacher training. The Wilkes had discovered that two years was a long time to wait for qualified Bible lecturers.

- include videos by prominent Bible scholars to begin each class. These experts could provide additional authority and content to the study, but the Wilkes also had another motive. Years before, they had led weekly group counseling for couples, and they began each session by playing a recorded lecture by a marriage expert. From that, they discovered how a listening experience helps to focus the group's attention and prepare group members for discussion.

After they had finished, the Wilkes waited for those gathered to comment. "Somebody said, 'That's what we need,' " Richard Wilke recalls. "And somebody else said, 'I like this, and I like that.' And then there was a silence, and Mr. Feaster, the president of the publishing house, said, 'Well, why don't we do it?' "

Nothing Short of a Miracle

Though the Wilkes still hadn't been asked to write the study, they were invited to lead a "consultation"—a publishing-house practice that draws together experts to brainstorm ideas for any planned product. Claude Young worked to make sure the group of twenty or so people represented the full spectrum of Christian theology. "We agreed we needed clergy and laity, ethnic minorities, theological people, intergenerational, men and women," says the former pastor.

The site for the overnight meeting was a Christian retreat center in Flower Mound, Texas, a farming community about thirty miles north of Dallas. The location was selected partly because of its proximity to Southern Methodist University's Perkins School of Theology, where two crucial voices served on the faculty—the late Albert Outler, perhaps the most renowned Methodist theologian at the time, and the late Dick Murray, a well-respected curriculum writer and professor of Christian education.

The two men drove out to Flower Mound together, Murray recalled shortly before his death in 2002. He and Outler both had attended dozens of similar get-togethers for one group or another over the years, and their experiences had left them both a bit jaded.

"Do you think we're going to do anything out here?" Outler asked.

"I don't know," Murray responded. "Usually don't."

"Then we probably won't," Outler said.

But what happened over the next twenty-four hours, Murray said, was nothing short of "a miracle." After the Wilkes introduced their ideas in the afternoon, a spirited discussion ensued long into the night. As ideas came up, they were jotted down on tacked-up sheets of newsprint. By the end of the evening, the room was wallpapered with notes. Into the wee hours, the Wilkes organized and distilled the scribbling. The next morning, they presented their summary to the group.

Claude Young cherishes the memory of the reaction. Despite the wide diversity of the group, "there was no disagreement at all," he says. "These were people who opposed one another philosophically, theologically, biblically, and socially. But when it came down to a Bible study that would inform all of us, there was complete agreement."

Both Outler and Murray contributed important refinements. Outler made a plea for each lesson to describe some aspect of human beings' sinful nature—the way people act outside of God's will. From this insight grew what would eventually set it apart from other studies—the idea of personal transformation. This study wouldn't simply teach the contents of the Bible; it would actively challenge people to become Christian disciples.

Murray's teaching strategies also permeate the final product, most notably his insistence that classes periodically break up into even smaller groups for more intimate reflection. Murray also is credited with the study's working title, BECOMING DISCIPLES THROUGH BIBLE STUDY, which later became its subtitle. The name, DISCIPLE, was the natural successor. (Richard Wilke eventually selected the red color for the study manual cover to symbolize the Passion of Jesus Christ, as well as the passion to become a disciple.)

Another noteworthy addition that came out of the consultation was the decision to let the Scriptures set the agenda of each lesson rather than picking out readings to fit predetermined topics. Everyone also agreed that the study be free of any denominational doctrine. This was going to be a product intended for all Christians.

Only a few more pieces were needed to complete the picture. Soon after the Flower Mound meeting, the Wilkes were asked to write the study manual. The choice was based on their ability to teach and communicate as well as their knowledge of the Bible. To help the couple navigate the intricacies of the text, two prominent scholars were enlisted—William Power, an Old Testament professor at Southern Methodist University, and Leander Keck, a New Testament professor who was the dean of Yale University Divinity School. Nellie Moser, who attended the consultation and eventually crafted the final proposal, signed on to edit the project.

The last major figure in the venture was added at an early planning session back in Nashville. The production team began trying to work out the particulars of training the study leaders, but no one in the room had any experience organizing a training event. Someone suggested bringing Wini Grizzle into the discussion. The former schoolteacher and businesswoman had joined the publishing house only a couple of months before to run training seminars for Sunday school teachers. Grizzle, who has the demeanor of a den mother and the business acumen of a corporate executive, entered the meeting knowing nothing about DISCIPLE. She left the meeting in charge of its training events.

A New Product, a New Approach

Customarily, the publishing house completes new products on a three-year timeline. But Richard Wilke pushed to keep the momentum going, and vice president Claude Young plotted a production schedule at a breakneck pace. Everything—writing, editing, printing, videotaping, marketing, training-event planning, and scheduling—would be completed in just fourteen months. The plan was to have the finished product in hand for the first training event in June 1987.

Back in Little Rock, the Wilkes set up shop in their home's book-lined study. Richard Wilke was still maintaining a full schedule as bishop, so the couple crammed their work into evenings and weekends.

The first step they took was to divide the Bible into reading assignments, then divide the assignments into weekly lessons. The study would cover more than 70 percent of Scripture in thirty-four weeks—roughly the length of a school year.

"Nellie was quite insistent that there would be at least three to five chapters of reading a day," Wilke recalls. "We had to figure out which chapters. Also, the lesson often didn't break right. For instance, the Creation story is all done in the first three chapters. Well, what else are you going to read that week? We ended up adding the Creation psalms and even passages from Job."

With a rough outline of the manual in hand, the couple consulted Power and Keck, as well as an extensive collection of reference works, to help them frame the commentary for each lesson. Wilke was the one who actually wrote the text, and he did so entirely in longhand (a secretary typed the final manuscript). Julia Wilke was rarely more than a few feet away doing research, lending counsel, and making suggestions. She also offered the first edit, a task that ranged from recommending word changes to rearranging whole sections with scissors and cellophane tape.

Moser began receiving portions of the manuscript in September 1986. A meticulous editor, she and her assistant Katherine Bailey double-checked every fact and ensured that every historical interpretation matched prevailing scholarship. Moser also wrote the guide for study leaders, identified the subjects for the ten-minute video presentations, and assembled the team of authoritative Bible experts and scholars to appear in them. She worked hard to create a list that reflected a diversity of Christian denominations, as well as ethnicity and gender. Among those who agreed to appear were Power, Keck, Outler, and of course, Wilke. Zan W. Holmes, Jr., a highly regarded Dallas minister with a distinctly sonorous voice, was selected to introduce each video segment. All traveled to Nashville for the videotaping.

Meanwhile, Wini Grizzle and her staff were making calls to churches around the country. They had their work cut out for them, trying to promote an untested product and a totally new approach. The study wouldn't be sold in bookstores, nor would it be available for individual use; only group sales were allowed. Besides that, leaders were strongly encouraged to enroll in an $800 training event that lasted three days. Unlike other seminars sponsored by the publishing house, these events would be held in hotels, not in churches or at camps. The decision, explains Grizzle, was all part of the effort "to make a statement that this was different. We wanted to raise the level of training. Corporations did it for things that were important. Why couldn't we do it in the church?"

A hotel setting also didn't encourage the come-and-go atmosphere of other locations. "We were reinforcing what we wanted to happen at the local church in their groups," Grizzle explains. "It wasn't a drop-in kind of Bible study. It was a very prayerful commitment. It required preparation. It required planning. So what we were trying to do at training was begin to change that mindset, so they could go back to their churches and say, 'This is different.' "

Initially, Grizzle's staff targeted ministers to take the training, with the hope that their commitment to a thirty-four-week study would lend it the necessary credibility. The expectation was for new leaders to emerge from these inaugural groups.

As news of the study spread, it was generally greeted with anticipation, says Grizzle. "We knew we were onto something big—real big," she says. "We were getting some very big churches, and people were saying this was exactly what they needed."

But there also was criticism, recalls Claude Young. Ministers objected to the cost of the material and the training, as well as to the amount of time the study would take. "They fussed and fussed and fussed," says Young. "We knew this was coming. But the truth of the matter is, very few churches don't have the money. They just want to spend it the way they want to spend it. The philosophy always was, If you don't make some sort of sacrifice, you won't get anything out of it."

Eventually, the publishing house established scholarships to assist churches that couldn't afford the study, as well as a program for larger churches to underwrite the cost for smaller churches. Free training also has been offered annually to seminary students, many of whom would likely receive their first appointment to a small church.

In the end, a total of 626 people, mostly ministers, signed up in 1987 for the first five training events, which were held in Atlanta, Chicago, Dallas, Denver, and the Los Angeles area. Everywhere they went, Grizzle and her team of trainers received a rousing response—as well as something else they had never expected. The people they were training wanted more. "In Atlanta they said they wanted a youth edition," says Grizzle. "Then in Denver someone stood up and asked, 'Will there be a "son of DISCIPLE"?' "

The Wilkes and Moser—and the rest of the publishing house for that matter—had thought their job was done. In fact, it was only beginning. If there was ever any doubt about how the Bible study would be received, it was laid to rest that autumn. "We began to get calls and letters from people who were just overwhelmed with what was happening in their groups, and they wanted us to know," Grizzle says. By the next spring, she recalls, "The phones were ringing off the hooks, with people asking, 'What's next?' "

Though Grizzle, Moser, the Wilkes, and others involved in DISCIPLE had confidence in the quality of their product, even they were caught off-guard by the emotional tenor of the response. And no wonder: Unknown to them, DISCIPLE had been introduced into a cresting wave of spiritual and social change that wouldn't be clearly identified by trend-watchers until the early 1990s. With a quiet sense of long-ing, more and more Americans were moving—and con-tinue to move—in two new and distinctive ways, and DISCIPLE just happened to overlap with both.

The first is "the desire for spiritual moorings," explains George Gallup, Jr., whose polling organization has been tracking trends in religion since 1935. The number of "peo-ple who want to experience spiritual growth has shot up" in recent decades. The second, he says, "is the desire to reach out to each other, to grow together."

In a landmark study in 1991, the George H. Gallup International Institute discovered that 40 percent of adult Americans belonged to some sort of small, supportive peer group. Of those, 60 percent were organized around issues of faith. In the years since, these numbers have continued to hold steady.

The latest insight into small groups, Gallup explains, "is that belonging comes before believing. Connecting comes first, and I think that's what happens with a lot of people. They're seeking a place to be themselves and learn and grow with others. And out of that, faith deepens."

Though little about this movement was obvious when DISCIPLE was introduced, the publishing house did recog-nize that a single Bible study was failing to satisfy a hungry market. In 1988, it introduced a youth version of DISCIPLE that featured less Bible reading, two fewer lessons, and questions oriented toward younger students. Then in 1989 a second consultation convened in Nashville to deal with the bigger issue: How do you create a sequel to a study that has already covered the entire Bible?

"The discussion went round and round," Richard Wilke recalls. "Someone said let's have a study of stewardship. Someone said we could study missions or we could study evangelism. The response was, those are topical and impor-tant, but that's not DISCIPLE."

Old Testament professor William Power finally broke the

impasse with what he thought was a casual observation. Traditionally, he said, the Hebrew Scriptures are divided into three parts: the Books of Moses (or Torah), the Prophets, and the Writings. All are contained in the Old Testament of the Bible, but with the exception of the first five books, they're in a completely different order.

The comment brought an unexpected clarity. Three subsequent studies could work their way back through the Bible with more depth. Gradually, the group identified a New Testament counterpart to each of the three parts of the Hebrew Scriptures:

- Genesis and Exodus tell the story of the beginning— of Creation and of the Hebrew people. The Gospel of Luke and Acts, both written by Luke, tell the story of the beginning of Christianity.

- Isaiah, Jeremiah, Hosea, and the other prophets call the rulers and their people to repentance. In Paul's many letters, repentance is a common theme. Also, biblical scholars traditionally interpret Paul's role as prophetic.

- The Writings—such as Psalms, Proverbs, Ecclesiastes, Job, and Ruth—all address issues of daily life, both large and small. In the New Testament, the Gospel of John deals with the purpose and meaning of life; the Letter of James presents practical advice on how to live a Christian life; and finally, that most mysterious of books, Revelation, offers a response to life under threat of persecution. The writer of Revelation also drew heavily on the Book of Daniel, which is among the Writings.

DISCIPLE had now become a four-part series, and the Wilkes and Moser all agreed to reprise their roles. The second study, INTO THE WORD INTO THE WORLD, was released in 1991 with a green cover to signify growth. The third study,

REMEMBER WHO YOU ARE, came out in 1996; its cover, purple, is the traditional color for repentance. The fourth study, UNDER THE TREE OF LIFE, was introduced in 2001 with a cover of gold, which alludes to passages in Proverbs and Revelation.

Each part in the series has come to be known more commonly by the order in which it first appeared—DISCIPLE 1, DISCIPLE 2, and so forth—even though they were never officially numbered. (The original study is intended to be taken first, but the others can be taken in any order.) The latter three each last for thirty-two weeks—two fewer than the first—to be better aligned with the length of a traditional school year, as well as to accommodate the lesser amount of reading.

Since the introduction of DISCIPLE, all four principals in the Bible study—the two Wilkes, Moser, and Grizzle—have had the opportunity to participate in a DISCIPLE class, and they've gotten to see its power for themselves. All remain in awe of what has been accomplished. "When any of us get together, one of us will inevitably say, 'God is in it,' " says Richard Wilke, "and the rest of us will say, 'That's the truth.' It has moved in areas and dimensions that only God could have placed it. Everyone understands that."

And this, says Wilke, is as it should be. In one of his favorite Bible passages, the story of Ezekiel and the valley of dry bones (Ezekiel 37), God tells Ezekiel to prophesy to the Word. When Ezekiel does, the bones come together, but still they are lifeless. And so God tells Ezekiel to prophesy to the spirit. "Everybody who talks about DISCIPLE speaks about the power of Scripture and the power of the spirit within the group," Wilke says. "That's how God said transformation would come—through the Word and through the Spirit."

CHAPTER THREE

WORD AND SPIRIT

andy Mann was absolutely clear about why she'd enrolled in DISCIPLE Bible study. And when it came her turn to introduce herself during the first class, she said so. "I'm just taking this to argue with my son more intelligently," declared the forty-nine-year-old former teacher.

Which came first—God or the human need for God? This was no "chicken or egg" question for the Colorado Springs woman. She was certain a book like the Bible was a wholly manmade tool, a sacred instruction manual for people to know how to get along in the world. But now her twenty-six-year-old son had become a fundamentalist Christian. He'd call her up from his home in North Carolina and quote her Scripture, trying to save her eternal soul. More and more, she felt woefully ill-equipped to refute his conclusions.

She did attend a Methodist church, mostly because it was her husband's denomination, although, she quickly adds, she enjoyed the minister's sermons. When she heard about a DISCIPLE class forming, she thought it sounded like a well-structured study. And so, in 1998, she bought a Bible and enrolled, as she might have enrolled in one of the classes she'd been taking for her master of arts degree at Colorado College. It was going to be an intellectual exercise.

And then, three weeks into the study, she felt something happening. She felt herself plunging—inexplicably, inescapably—into the mystery of faith. "It's just . . . ," Mann says, struggling to describe her response to the Bible. " 'True' is not right . . . " She stops, then starts again. "There's a certain, 'Yes, that's right.' When you read these passages in the Bible and really get into them, you have an understanding of all time and all people, and you feel a kind of infinite connection that just can't be human. . . . It just melted away all my doubts and old understandings."

Like so many others who have taken DISCIPLE, Mann had an epiphany about the Bible. She realized it is more than stories, more than history, and certainly more than an instruction manual. As the late theologian Albert Outler says in one of the DISCIPLE videotapes, the best reason for reading the Bible is that "somewhere, somehow [you will] hear the Word of God."

Since DISCIPLE was introduced in 1987, hundreds of thousands of people in the United States and around the world have felt that euphoric sense of discovery—that sense, says Sandy Mann, that "you don't own the Bible; the Bible owns you." In daily readings and weekly meetings, they have studied, discussed, and discerned God's Word together; and they have come away with a new understanding of God's hold on their lives.

"Do not conform any longer to the pattern of this world," Paul wrote in Romans 12:2, "but be transformed by the renewing of your mind. Then you will be able to test and approve what God's will is—his good, pleasing and perfect will" (NIV).

Today, this is what Mann finds at the center of her focus,

far more than any differences she may still have with her son. Granted, the two continue to have lively discussions, and Mann says she still doesn't agree with his theology. Yet she believes they are now on "the same team," though playing different positions. "What sustains me now," she says, "is the belief that there's a power greater than me."

Unexpected Insights

What is this curious power of the Bible? As Christians through the ages have concluded, whatever it is, it has been created by God. But connecting with that power often depends as much on how Scripture is encountered as on the words themselves. Interestingly, Mann was already familiar with many of the Bible's stories before she took DISCIPLE; she had taught the Bible as literature to junior high students in social studies back in the early 1970s. But not until DISCIPLE did she realize she needed the guidance of a study to absorb the Bible's spiritual impact.

Over the years, DISCIPLE has attracted students with a wide range of biblical experience. Many haven't come to it since children's Sunday school. Others have waded through its pages on their own. Some have heard the words only in recitation during Sunday morning services. Some are familiar with nothing more than the Christmas and Easter stories. But no matter the DISCIPLE student's background, surprises always seem to be in store during the course of study. In DISCIPLE circles, these are often referred to as "aha!" moments—those unexpected instants of new insight. Sometimes they become turning points in faith.

Elaine Klessig was leading a DISCIPLE class in the study of Job when she unsuspectingly knocked the spiritual slats out from under one of her students. Linda Hollenbeck, a forty-year-old homemaker and mother of two boys, knew nothing about the Bible until adulthood; her introduction was an earlier Bible study with a group of neighborhood friends who tended toward a literal view of Scripture. Now, when Klessig suggested that Job probably never existed—that most scholars believe his life of misery is almost certainly a dramatized fiction—Hollenbeck suddenly burst into tears. She haltingly explained that she believed every word in the Bible was written by God. Didn't that mean everything was fact? How could a made-up story just be thrown in?

"It seemed to her it wasn't God's book anymore," recalls Klessig, who has led several DISCIPLE classes at a United Methodist church in Rolling Hills Estates, California. "So we had quite an emotional night that night. We needed everybody's input just to reassure her it was O.K. to feel this way. We told her, 'You're going to learn more about how this Bible came together, but it still comes from God.' "

Looking back on that evening in 1995, Hollenbeck now realizes how unformed her faith was before DISCIPLE. "Most people who read the Bible," she contends, "are not that sophisticated. Most are searching and longing; they're just everyday folk, . . . and I guess I was one of those people. Who was going to explain to me that this story wasn't real, but that it's still a symbol of the strength someone can truly have in their faith?"

At a later session, another student—an engineer who usually took an intellectual approach to the Bible—helped Hollenbeck's understanding with a single comment. "He said, 'One thing I know for sure is that there was a spark that started everything, and that light is God,'" she recalls. "I just loved that visual, because that was his way of accepting that he didn't know all the *whys* and *whats*. He just knew there was a spark. And I thought, there was a spark! It made a lot of sense to me."

Hollenbeck went on to co-lead a DISCIPLE class with Klessig, who today refers to her friend as a "kitchen-sink theologian" because of her uncomplicated way of bringing the Bible "down to her home and to her family."

Even though she has led a DISCIPLE class almost every year since 1989, Diana Facemyer says she has never failed to be amazed by the insights that come to her when she does the assignments again. "The interesting thing about Bible study," says the United Methodist pastor in Glen Ellyn, Illinois, "is that every time you reread the most familiar parts, you yourself are different, so you hear and see things in the Bible differently." When she was in her twenties, she says, she was repelled by the story in John 4 about Jesus and the Samaritan woman at the well. In their meeting, Jesus shocks the woman by recounting her jaded past. "I couldn't imagine how horrifying this experience must have been—to have this terrible secret exposed by him," says Facemyer. But when Facemyer came across the story almost thirty years later in DISCIPLE Bible study, "I realized that it's a completely liberating thing—to give up your secrets and live the truth. Now, as an older person, I love that story. . . . I am that woman who is liberated by Christ in that encounter."

The Sum of All Its Parts

The writings in the Bible span thousands of years; they feature stories that are fantastic, troubling, profound, perplexing. There are miracles and disasters, wild dreams and veiled prophecy, kings and paupers, virgins and harlots. The Bible is actually a vast collection of books, yet somehow it is the sum of all its parts—a concept that's often difficult to grasp without a broad overview. Many Christians, if they go to the Bible at all, have a tendency to skip over the Old Testament and concentrate on Jesus' life in the Gospels. But rarely has a student come away from DISCIPLE without an appreciation for the entire text.

"I was one of those people who didn't understand the real relevance of the Old Testament," says Rusty Gordon, who has taken DISCIPLE at Roswell United Methodist

Church in Roswell, Georgia. "I looked at the Old Testament as the stories that weren't good enough to make the New Testament."

But as his DISCIPLE class plowed into the first books of the Bible in 1990, Gordon was struck by how God continually worked to relate to the chosen people. Jesus' appearance in the New Testament, Gordon concluded, was simply a continuation of God's desire for that human relationship. "One is in a corporate context, and the other is in a personal context," says Gordon, an Atlanta business executive. "The interesting thing for me is the fact that the Holy Spirit is extremely active in both cases."

Once Tom Edmondson, a DISCIPLE student in Leawood, Kansas, grasped the persistence of God's desire for human relationship, his whole reason for taking the course shifted. The thirty-year-old telecommunications manager signed up for the Bible study in 1999, he says, "on a search for answers." But soon that changed to being "on a search to grow closer to God." In the Old Testament, Edmondson found God to be amazingly patient with the flawed patriarchs Abraham and Jacob. "They weren't exactly upstanding folks," he says. "In fact, they were pretty devious. . . . It's just unbelievable how much God will forgive and forgive and forgive. Yes, there is an absolute right and wrong, and God is very clear about what he expects, and there will eventually be an accounting. But God gives so many chances."

Because of DISCIPLE, Edmondson says his daily prayer has changed from "God, I really need this" to "God, I am yours; what can I do to please you today?" "I give up my right to be selfish and ambitious," he says. "I give up my will to God's will. I understand that the more we do that, the more joy there is, and the more peace there is in our lives."

Larry Harris, a DISCIPLE leader in Pocatello, Idaho, is another who has been drawn to the common themes in both testaments. "What's been the most eye-opening to me is how I've come to a deeper understanding of the faith—and the faith story—that's expressed in the Old Testament," says Harris, who is the dean of education at Idaho State University. "Those stories are so vitally important as we try to understand what's in the New Testament." Especially stirring to Harris are the hopeful verses in the book of Isaiah, such as 60:2, that composer George Frederick Handel used in his epic choral work, *The Messiah*: "For, behold, the darkness shall cover the earth, and gross darkness the people: but the Lord shall arise upon thee, and his glory shall be seen upon thee" (KJV). Says Harris: "You have to work to understand that bad things happen, and God lets those things happen, but God is still there. Yes, there is a rock—a solid piece of faith—that will be there."

That's Revolutionary!

Many newcomers to the Old Testament are stunned by the wrath of God's judgment; from one book to the next, death, destruction, and exile seem to be God's disciplinary measures of choice. Or at least that's how it seemed initially to Claudia Roberts when she took Disciple in 1999. But the Portland, Oregon, vocational counselor gradually changed her perspective. "It wasn't until I read the Old Testament that I realized the New Testament was being written to help the Jewish people understand how Christ fit in the picture," she says. "Jesus knew it very well, and when he told his disciples at the Last Supper, 'This is the bread of my body and this wine is my blood,' he knew exactly what he was saying in terms of the Hebrew sacrificial system, and the people he was saying it to did, too. It took me until I was fifty years old to understand that connection. It means that our God today is the same God as always—that there wasn't a God of the Old Testament who was blood-thirsty, mean, and vicious, and a God of the New Testament who was beneficent, loving, and kind. It's just that the cultures were different. That allows me to accept and understand that God has remained constant from Genesis to Jesus, and certainly God has remained constant from Jesus to now."

Once she entered the Gospels, Roberts found more surprises in store, this time about Jesus. "You grow up with an image that he was this passive, itinerant preacher wandering around the countryside saying kind things to people," she says. "But I remember making notes in my Bible that said, 'My gosh, that's revolutionary! No wonder he upset people!' He really was much more of a radical, and what he offered to people was so tremendously different from what they'd been taught—not that it was a different message from the one that God had been trying to convey, but it was certainly different from the forms of Hebrew worship."

Like many DISCIPLE students, Roberts has enhanced her Bible study experience by developing a routine to go along with her daily reading. Whether in early morning or in the evening, she fixes a cup of tea and puts on a tape of soothing contemporary Christian music. Then she takes a seat on her living-room couch, where she can see the camellias and dogwood trees out the window. It doesn't take long for her black-and-white cat, Timmy, to find her lap. Roberts says she refuses to watch the clock as she studies. "I find I get more caught up in it and lost in it, and I stay with it until I'm at a point I want to stop," she says.

The way she reads the Bible isn't all that has changed over time; she also has developed a confidence in her own biblical interpretations. "When I started out," she says, "I spent as much time reading Bible commentaries as I did reading the Bible. I don't exactly know when it took place, but I've finally been able to let go of understanding the Scripture only in terms of how other people interpret it, and I'm able to trust my own sense of what I'm getting out of it. That's been very liberating."

Solace Amid Upheaval

The mysterious power of the Bible doesn't lie solely in the discernment of God's Word; it can also be in the timing. Most people come to DISCIPLE seeking some sort of guidance for their everyday lives. But during thirty-four weeks of study, a lot can happen to participants: Turning points can appear. Personal crises can arise. And often, in the midst of such upheaval, DISCIPLE students discover that Scripture is speaking to them with extraordinary resonance.

When Tait Berge enrolled in a DISCIPLE class at his Colorado Springs church in 1996, he was a young man already in anguish. A twenty-three-year-old college student with cerebral palsy, he had known for months that his service dog, Nouveau—his helper who literally opened doors for him along with dozens of other tasks—was going to be retired. The golden retriever had developed aggressive behavior that wasn't responding to training. In their seven years together, Berge and the dog had been inseparable. Nouveau had done more than give Berge his freedom; the dog had become a part of him. "I wanted to trust God," Berge, whose speech is limited by his condition, wrote in his self-published autobiography. "I wanted to believe that God knew what was best for me and Nouveau, but I couldn't let myself believe that."

Berge, who relies on a battery-powered wheelchair, searched for comfort during the first four weeks of DISCIPLE class, but he remained shy and withdrawn; he chose to listen to the discussion rather than join in by typing on his laptop computer or attempting to speak. Then, in the fifth week, the saga of the Hebrews' exodus from Egypt unfolded; it was a familiar story to Berge, but somehow God's command to a hesitant Moses in Exodus 4:11-12 had special significance as he heard it read aloud during class: "The LORD said to him, 'Who gave man his mouth? Who makes him deaf or mute? Who gives him sight or makes him blind? Is it

55

not I, the LORD? Now go; I will help you speak and will teach you what to say' " (NIV).

In the moment he heard those verses, "I finally found that spirit of God that I needed," says Berge. With or without Nouveau, he already had been liberated by God. With or without his dog, he knew he would never be alone. That evening, Berge spoke in class for the first time, and despite his struggle with the words, "everyone understood everything that I said." He talked about his disability and about the pain of losing his dog. Afterward, the others gathered around him and offered a blessing. A month later, Berge was able to say good-by to Nouveau and begin his training with a new dog. His DISCIPLE lessons, of course, continued. "I felt like I finally found my medicine," he writes of the Bible study in his autobiography, *My Exodus*. "I just needed God and his Word."

For Lynda Rhodes, Scripture didn't merely intersect with her life; it came at her with cyclone force. In 1995, the forty-eight-year-old artist took DISCIPLE at her Parkersburg, West Virginia, church seeking "a closer relationship with the Lord." A former fashion model, Rhodes is a tall and striking woman who, by outward appearance, seemed to have an easy life. Inside, though, she was carrying a lifetime of pain. Raised by bickering parents, she now was the primary caretaker for her ailing—and angry—father. Despite the daily stress, Rhodes prided herself in keeping a sunny exterior. "I've always tried to be a positive person," she says. "You try to make the best of it. You might be depressed, but you don't want to carry it out to everybody else."

Week after week, Rhodes felt nourished by the Scripture readings, but never so much as when she arrived at a lesson on Psalms. As she read the poetry that affirms God's abiding love and protection, she suddenly and inexplicably dissolved into tears. "I was just sobbing," she recalls, "and I thought, what is this? What is coming out of me?" Then just as suddenly, the tears stopped and a feeling of peace washed over her. From out of nowhere, a thought rushed into her mind, telling her, "I am with you now; I was with you then." Rhodes has no other explanation than that it came from God. At that moment she knew her painful past had finally been put to rest; she also knew God was now giving her the strength to endure her father's illness. In her study manual that evening, she copied down a portion of Psalm 40:

"I waited patiently for the LORD;
   he turned to me and heard my cry.
He lifted me out of the slimy pit,
   out of the mud and mire;
he set my feet on a rock
   and gave me a firm place to stand.
He put a new song in my mouth,
   a hymn of praise to our God" (40:1-3, NIV).

Since then Rhodes's father has died, and she has taken on the trying chore of caring for her mother, who is in poor health. Rhodes's younger sister has asked in amazement how she can manage the task. "I say, 'It's not me; it's the Lord in me that gives me compassion for her. The Lord is my strength. He's the one who gets me through this.' "

When Barry Trantham, a forty-four-year-old loan officer in Flushing, Michigan, enrolled in his DISCIPLE class in 1996, he had no idea it would prepare him for one of the toughest decisions he'd have to make in his life. At the course's start, Trantham admits, his faith wasn't that strong. But as the weeks passed and he heard how his classmates' prayer requests were being answered, he had to sit up and take notice. His own ninety-seven-year-old grandmother was quite ill; she had been a strong and loving presence throughout Trantham's life, and he couldn't bear the thought of losing her. And so, each week, he prayed for her health to improve.

Once into the Gospels, the class at Flushing United

Methodist Church studied the story of Jesus' raising Lazarus from the dead; the discussion turned to the topic of loved ones' dying. "We talked about . . . what a horrible time it was for us," recalls Trantham, "because we want these people with us, not with God." A few days later, he visited his grandmother in the nursing home. Sitting next to her bed, he asked how she was doing. She answered flatly, "O.K."

He immediately tried to cheer her. "You keep looking this good," he cajoled, "you'll get to go home."

His grandmother wasn't having it. "I'm not sure I want to go home," she told him. To Trantham, it seemed she was almost willing herself to die.

At the next DISCIPLE class, he shocked the other students during prayer requests. "I'm changing my prayer for my grandmother," he announced. "I'm praying for whatever's best for her, not for me."

Less than a week later, he got a call from the nursing home. An infection was sweeping through his grandmother's body; Trantham's father couldn't be reached, and a family decision had to be made quickly. All Trantham had to say was yes, and she would be transferred to the hospital, where heroic measures could be taken to try to save her life. "Right then, I had a peace come over me," says Trantham, "and I said, 'That's not what she wants.' " As he said it, he could feel a weight slip from his shoulders. Two days later, his grandmother died.

Looking back, Trantham believes that God did answer his prayer. "He was holding her here until I was ready to let her go," he says. And he says, he wouldn't have been ready without the Bible study. "I feel that God wanted me in that DISCIPLE class."

CHAPTER FOUR

TRANSFORMED LIVES

When Jesus beckoned Simon Peter and Andrew to come and be his disciples, the two brothers were going about what they probably had done most days of their lives—tossing their fishing nets into the waters of Galilee. But without hesitation, they dropped everything to follow Jesus. The scene played out again when Jesus saw two more brothers, James and John, in a boat with their nets. He called, and they came.

What does it mean to become a disciple?

As these two episodes from the Gospels illustrate, it's as simple as leaving behind the old ways for the new. It's following the Living Word on faith.

But that was then, and this is now. Modern-day life is a tangle of obligations and activities—of work and family and rush-hour traffic in between. There are deadlines to be met, bills to be paid, housework to be done. Forget about trying to get ahead. It's hard enough just to stay even. In this day and age, people simply couldn't drop everything and follow on faith. Could they?

Becoming a Force for Good

Snapshot of Laura Alexander Elliott in 1990: Corporate climber. Recognition-seeker. Perfectionist. Thirty years old and already a marketing officer at a big bank. Her historian husband is the one who spends more time with their infant son; she's the one with the bigger salary, the benefits, the one-way ticket on the fast track.

Religion? Sure, she goes to church, but that's because her parents did. That's what families do. As for the Bible, well, that's just the book those annoying fundamentalists like to wave in folks' faces to make them feel bad. Surely there's nothing in it for her.

Snapshot of Laura Alexander Elliott ten years later: Charity worker. Community volunteer. Servant for social justice. Forty years old and the public information officer for a nonprofit agency that deals with homelessness. It's a part-time job that gives her more hours with her husband and two sons, now ages six and ten.

Religion? She's starting to take classes at a divinity school so she can more fully understand God's claim on her life. As for the Bible, well, allow Elliott to describe what happened during one of her first DISCIPLE classes in 1990 at her Winston-Salem, North Carolina, church.

"We were talking about the Creation story," she recalls, "and I felt like I was traveling at a high rate of speed through a tunnel. At the end, all the lights went on and everything opened up in my head. . . . And here was my faith in front of me. I understood it now. I saw that I had been listening to the fundamentalists' point of view on the Bible, and it had driven me away from my faith. . . . I hadn't been looking at it for myself."

Elliott had tagged along with her husband to the class at Centenary United Methodist Church. He was the one with the interest; she had no idea what, if anything, she'd get out of it. After growing up in a Christian home, she felt she already had a strong moral foundation. She knew, of course, what sin was. But once she began the weekly study and started reading the Bible for the first time, it dawned on her that something had been missing from her upbringing. Yes, she knew what she shouldn't do—but what was it that she was supposed to do? "I began to realize," she says, "how I could be not just a good person, but a force for good."

Before DISCIPLE she had spent her years in a pew listening to the Christmas and Easter stories, but she had never thoughtfully examined the life that came in between. Now, as the class entered the New Testament, she was becoming acquainted with Jesus, a flesh-and-blood man who lifted up the poor, broke bread with outcasts, and preached in parables about justice and reconciliation. When she reached the parable of the good Samaritan, the familiar story no longer seemed an unsophisticated lesson on being kind to one's neighbor. Now it was a complex command to reach out and embrace the most despised and disenfranchised in society, a command that held the promise of change for all involved.

After completing DISCIPLE, she felt an immediate urge to make some sort of response, so she decided to lead a class herself. Other, more life-altering stirrings would occur more gradually.

One day, months later, a sign-up sheet to deliver meals to shut-ins landed on her desk at work. It was the sort of thing that she'd seen dozens of times before, the sort of thing that always made her think how nice it would be to "do good." Except this time she did it.

Driving the Meals on Wheels route once a month only churned her desire to do more. She volunteered for a local commission on human relations and for the United Way. At her church, she served as chair of the DISCIPLE coordinating committee and later as a member of the council of ministries. At her bank, she began focusing extra attention on one small piece of her marketing work—upholding the Community Reinvestment Act, a federal regulation that requires banks to market to low-income communities. Even as she was promoted into positions with more responsibility, she insisted this duty move with her. "People were amazed," she says. "They were curious about why I was so attached to it." How, in a culture steeped in profits and earnings, could she begin to explain her deepening commitment to economic equality?

While in meditation one day in 1992, she was shocked to feel God tugging her toward becoming involved in politics. At the time, she wasn't even registered to vote. But she had been following the ongoing presidential campaign, so she showed up at a local headquarters to stuff envelopes and make telephone calls. She eventually moved on to help a mayoral hopeful win her election. Through these contacts, she was called on to do even more volunteer work in civic and local political affairs.

Politics to some people, she knows, might seem the antithesis of godly work. But her experience taught her otherwise. "Politics has done so much for me in terms of not just tolerating people who are different but really embracing them," she says. "It's very much a part of my faith growth and understanding."

In 1997 Elliott's bank underwent a merger, and she was transferred to yet another new position. This time, her sole responsibility was marketing the bank's brokerage services to its most affluent customers. Immediately she felt out of place. Everything in her life since DISCIPLE had been pointing her toward helping people in need. But here she was, peddling to people who had more than enough.

For two years, "I tried every way to Sunday to avoid what God was trying to say to me, which is, 'I have something different for you in your life.' " When she finally decided to look for another job, she sent resumes to several area banks. But she also resolved to look for ways to use the skills she had developed in her church and community work. "And that," she says, "is where things opened up."

At the time she was serving on the board of a nonprofit agency that offers comprehensive services to return the homeless to self-sufficiency. That's where she learned about its need for a marketing and public-information officer. Though the position paid significantly less than what she was making, the shorter work week would allow her more time with her family. In the summer of 1999, at age thirty-eight, she took the job. Her banking colleagues thought she was going through a midlife crisis; Elliott saw it a different way. "It was all about my faith development," she says.

At times the work has been arduous—she's been the agency spokeswoman in wrangles over city funding—but it's satisfying in a way that banking rarely was. Still, she hasn't yet arrived at her planned destination. Next stop—a divinity degree at Wake Forest University. "It will take me forever," she says, "but the ultimate culmination will be some sort of certification in the church." With that in hand, she hopes to pursue a career in outreach ministry.

When Elliott reflects on her corporate years, she marvels at the turns her life has taken. "I used to worry myself sick about what I did and whether I had done it well enough," she says. "I was a perfectionist, and I always wanted recognition, too."

"It was ultimately my faith, through DISCIPLE, that motivated me to look at my life and think about what I really wanted to do. I needed the motivation to do what God was calling me to do. . . . I now believe God calls us to be faithful, not successful."

A Marriage Resurrected

It's after 9:00 P.M., and Todd Martin is driving a dark highway somewhere in northern Mississippi, passing the time talking on his cell phone about his faith. He's headed home to a Memphis, Tennessee, suburb after a long day of sales meetings. Tomorrow he'll be back out on the road before 7:00 A.M., on his way to still more distant meetings. But tonight—tonight he'll be in his own bed, sleeping next to his wife, and to Martin, that's the way it should be.

That's not the way it has always been, however. "I know God pursues every single one of us," he says, his lively drawl accompanied by the telephone's soft static. "He doesn't want one person to perish."

He knows the Bible well enough to mention that he's paraphrasing 2 Peter 3:9: "The Lord is not slow in keeping his promise, as some understand slowness. He is patient with you, not wanting anyone to perish, but everyone to come to repentance" (NIV).

As far as Todd Martin is concerned, God's patience finally paid off for him in the fall of 1997. After a couple of false starts, that's when the thirty-four-year-old sales representative finally committed to taking DISCIPLE Bible study. Before then, Martin had been doing a pretty good job of running away from God, though he really didn't understand that until much later.

At the time, he was living on the road, from hotel room to hotel room. Even when he could be home with his wife and their three young daughters, he was still coming up with excuses to stay away. He spent more hours than he'd like to count drinking too much and frequenting strip clubs. When he was home, he walled himself off from his family. While they sat at the dining table, he ate his meals in front of the television set. On Sunday mornings, he usually stayed in bed while they went to their church in nearby Collierville. "Every reason to not be happy in church, I would find," he says.

His wife, Marti, a high school math teacher, coped with the distance with silence and prayer. "Not like I should have," she admits. "Sometimes I was praying out of anger.

But I was praying that God would hold us together. . . . I knew unless God got involved it wasn't going to last."

In 1994 Martin impulsively signed up for a DISCIPLE class, then crossed his name off the list. The next year he enrolled again but never came to class. Two years later, though, he felt a tug that he couldn't ignore. This time, he signed up and showed up. "I didn't know it then," he says, "but God was talking to me a lot, and I was beginning to listen."

His barriers didn't fall quickly, though. In class, "I tended to be very judgmental," he says, "because it was easy to say, 'They're wrong and I'm not.' " But week by week, the Scriptures began to chip away at his defenses. On February 8, 1998—Martin remembers the exact date—he awoke to another Sunday when he didn't want to go to church. But somehow he managed to make his way with his family to the sanctuary. "I sat down and said, 'Darn it, I'm not enjoying this.' I was in the worst mood."

The topic of the sermon that morning was "Experiencing God"; the Scripture was taken from the book of Jonah. Martin fished around for a pen and began to make notes on his bulletin. Suddenly, he felt that he and the minister were the only ones in the room. "He talked about how Jonah had run from the Lord, and really and truly, at that moment, I was convicted by the Holy Spirit. I knew my life was in ruins, and I'd run away from God."

After church, Martin pulled into his driveway, sent his family into the house, then sat in the car and wept.

Marti Martin remembers when her husband walked into the kitchen, his eyes red from crying. "He told me about how much the sermon touched him," she says, "and he just wanted to stand there and hug."

From that moment on, Martin hungrily devoured the Bible as if he'd been starving for God's Word all his life. "I couldn't read enough, I couldn't study enough," he says. "I burned through DISCIPLE."

His heart and eyes now opened, he examined his life in a

new and sobering light. He saw how his selfish whims had laid claim to his soul. He saw that his marriage and family life were in shambles. "When I sat back and looked at where my life had gone the last seven or eight years," he says, "it was just wrong. . . . That was not what I was here for, and I knew it."

Why had he distanced himself so much from God? Paul's words in Romans 7:15-25 offered Martin insight, solace, and hope: "I do not understand what I do. For what I want to do I do not do, but what I hate I do. And if I do what I do not want to do, I agree that the law is good. As it is, it is no longer I myself who do it, but it is sin living in me. . . . Who will rescue me from this body of death? Thanks be to God—through Jesus Christ our Lord! So then, I myself in my mind am a slave to God's law, but in the sinful nature a slave to the law of sin" (NIV).

Martin was determined to put his life in order. Together, he and his wife realized they had to make a choice: Get a divorce or get help. They chose marriage counseling and stuck with it for eighteen months. "There was a lot of trying and a lot of crying and a lot of forgiveness," Martin says.

Day by day, the changes began to accumulate. The drinking and the clubbing stopped. More and more often, Martin decided a couple of hours' drive to get home was better than a lonely night in a hotel. At least three nights a week, his schedule was adjusted so he could be with his family in time for dinner; he now was taking his place at the table. He made a conscious effort to get to know his daughters better and to plan family activities. And whenever they could, he and his wife took time in the morning for devotion and prayer together.

In search of more spiritual renewal, Martin took a Walk to Emmaus, a three-day retreat intended to draw participants closer to God. Afterward, several men from the retreat formed a weekly "accountability" group for fellowship and support.

As Martin's faith blossomed, so did an impulse toward service. He volunteered for committees at his church, Collierville United Methodist. He turned his computer skills to building Web sites for the church and for the Memphis church community's Walk to Emmaus program; he also volunteered to be the "ring servant" for the United Methodist Church web ring, which includes more than 450 congregations around the world.

Before his day of reckoning, Martin had never given more than $100 a year to the church. He vowed to do better, and his gifts have steadily increased. His goal is one day to give 10 percent of his income, the tithe called for in Scripture.

If God had not jolted him that day in 1998, says Martin, he knows his life would have continued its slide. "I'm not going to tell you I've walked a perfect way since," he says, "but it's been very different. We're all on a path to perfection. Will we get there? No. But God continues to work on us."

In 2001 the Martins celebrated their fifteenth wedding anniversary. They decided to celebrate the occasion with a solemn renewal of their marriage vows. Their children and a few close friends joined them in the circle with their pastor.

"It was Todd's idea," says Marti Martin. "We talked about how important it was for us to be ready and willing and committed to place God first. We have to remember that God is the foundation and groundwork for everything we do."

During the ceremony, the Martins exchanged the familiar vows; then all the participants took communion and prayed at the altar rail. "We renewed our love before God," says Martin, "and we asked God to join us. When we were married the first time, we said all those things, but we didn't mean it. God did his part, but we didn't do ours."

Though a whole phase of their lives was now behind them, his wife couldn't help but look back one last time. "It was very touching to sit there and think about the first fifteen years and all the good times and all the bad times," she says, "and realize we're both willing to commit and renew and just keep going. . . . Because of God, we are truly married now."

Going About the Business of Faith

Late one night in the fall of 1987, Steve Tucker opened his Bible to the DISCIPLE assignment for the day: Genesis 28–33. As the thirty-five-year-old Atlanta salesman read the vivid account of Jacob's wrestling match with God, he easily pictured the scene—two figures locked in fierce struggle, neither letting go, neither giving in. But in the role of the rebellious patriarch, Tucker was shocked to see a familiar face. It was his own.

For years Tucker believed he knew how to live right. He'd surrounded himself with the evidence—a loving wife, two beautiful young daughters, a high-powered career, a six-figure salary, and all the luxuries that ample supplies of money could buy. Tucker thought he was a Christian, too; after all, he was at church on Sunday, wasn't he?

But now, with this Bible scene filling his mind and the self-recognition piercing his heart, he knew otherwise. He knew—just like Jacob—he'd been trying to exert his own will over God's. He'd been doing things his way, not God's way. Tears streamed down his face as he finally realized why he had felt empty for so long.

Tucker was in the mountains of western North Carolina at the time, serving as a sponsor for a church youth retreat. Early the next morning, he rose for a walk around a lake. Pausing under the canopy of a cypress tree, he sat and started to pray. Soon he was praying as he never had before. Like Jacob, he told God he was ready to surrender. "Lord," he prayed, "I'll try it your way. Just give me another chance."

Immediately, Tucker set about to reorder his life. In the ensuing months, he plowed through the rest of the Bible study, searching for God's plan for him. Eventually, he felt he had found it: He believed God was calling him into the ordained ministry.

In the summer of 1988, Tucker moved quickly. He enrolled in the fall semester of a local seminary. He resigned his sales position at an Atlanta real estate development company, and he put his finances in order. All he had to do was wait for classes to start. Then his wife, Connie, asked him a simple question.

"You'll have enough time for your studies, and you'll have enough time to support us financially," she said, "but have you figured out how you're going to have enough time to be a father to our daughters?"

Tucker now chuckles at the memory. "We'd prefer God to speak to us through a burning bush," he says, "rather than through our wives."

Once again, he sought refuge in prayer. He had to admit it. He hadn't figured everything out. He'd gotten caught up in wanting to show God what he could do, "as opposed to surrendering my life so God could work through me." His seminary plans evaporated. But now what was he going to do?

The first step, he decided, was to examine what he could do. He already knew his gift lay in his entrepreneurial skills. Why had God given him this gift, he wondered, if God had not intended him to use it? Was it so unthinkable to live out God's plan in the business world?

"That was when I began to recognize that if Christ's word had any meaning at all, there had to be a way to apply the things we talked about on Sunday to what we did on Monday and Tuesday and every other day of the week," says Tucker, who attends a Baptist church. "I felt my calling was to figure a way to work it out."

Days, weeks, months passed. Tucker struck out on his own, piecing together residential-development deals. But he also was dedicating himself to a whole new battery of daily disciplines—praying, reading Scripture, keeping a prayer journal.

Within a couple of years, he felt he had prepared himself both professionally and spiritually to launch his own company. No doubt Jesus was speaking metaphorically when he preached about the wise man building his house on the rock, but Steve Tucker took the counsel a bit more literally. His new business, set upon a foundation of faith, would be homebuilding. "I knew I wanted to build houses and grow organizationally in a way to strive to honor God and his glory," he says, "and that's what I wrote down in a mission statement."

Five years later, in 2000, Custom One Homes was a success on any business scale—a multimillion-dollar corporation completing up to three hundred new houses a year, counted among the top twenty homebuilders in the Atlanta market. But few successful businesses could boast of the practices that Tucker had put into place.

What does this faith-centered corporation look like?

At Custom One, all earnings are tithed, and most business meetings start with a blessing. A staff member leads Bible studies and takes employee prayer requests on company time. Bibles and other books on faith are given away by the hundreds to customers. Employees get extra time off for important family events; salespeople with children have the option of working thirty-five hours a week (albeit for less pay). Once a year, operations shut down so the core staff of about twenty can take a company-financed mission trip to work in an impoverished area. Regular employee retreats have themes like "God's Vision for Your Life: How Does It Apply to Us Corporately and Individually?"

Custom One's two-story headquarters was constructed to resemble a family home—with brick and shutters on the outside and warm, comfortable furnishings inside. Prominently posted on its walls, as well as in every sales office and construction trailer, is the set of corporate values:

"Integrity, trustworthiness, the Golden Rule, honest and truthful communications, servant leadership and stewardship."

Newspaper want ads seeking new workers entreat: "If honesty, integrity, and the time you spend with your family and with your faith are more important than your job, you may fit in the Custom One team." The ads are a rarity, though; the employee turnover rate sits at about 5 percent annually.

At the hub of it all is Tucker, a tall, trim man who sees no conflict between his faith and his profit motive. "We have to make a profit to stay in business so we can serve God with our prosperity," he says. "I can't help God if we're not making a profit."

Tucker is the first to admit he's made mistakes as he's worked to put his Christianity into business practice. During the first year, he says, he hired and fired fifteen employees. All of them, he says, had professed to believing in the corporate values, "but there's a big difference between believing them and upholding them in your life." God has since helped him become more discerning in his hiring choices, he says. Product quality also proved to be an issue in the beginning. "We weren't meeting customers' expectations," says Tucker. "I finally had to stop all new construction, and I said, 'We've got to go back and do what we said we'd do.' From that point forward, we came up with a zero-tolerance policy."

While Tucker asks a lot of his work force, he demands even more of himself. He stays attuned to God through daily prayer, as well as through a night of solitude once a week on his forty-foot sloop anchored at an Atlanta-area lake. Into the wee hours, he reads the Bible, writes in his journal, and prays, sometimes facedown on the floor. He also blocks out a third of his work hours for "spiritual mentoring" of other businessmen in small get-togethers. "The goal," he says, "is to help them appropriate a heart for what

God is doing in their life. I find my role is not to tell them what they're supposed to do, but to point out what God is already doing in their lives so they can make their own decision about what the Holy Spirit is calling them to do."

From time to time, customers take note that they're dealing with a different kind of company. Tucker welcomes their reactions. "Then we have a chance to say, 'Let me tell you what the Lord has done in my life and what we're doing about it,' " he says. "People say, 'You guys seem to really care.' Yeah, we do. That's why we work in a company that really does care. I believe Christ provides an example for living our life and building our business."

As Custom One Homes evolves, so does Tucker's way of managing it. God, he says, is hardly finished with either the company or its founder. One of his ongoing struggles has been over deciding how to limit his own worldly wants. "It's really heady stuff," he says, "and God in his wisdom and love chose to deal with me on it. He began asking me and my wife to determine how much was enough, and we have, and we're learning to live within that amount. If we have to pay more and more attention to our material desires, we're taking our attention off God. I've seductively slipped and slid into that mindset over the years, and I would not tell you that I'm out of the woods yet."

Every day, though, offers him a new opportunity to submit to God's will. "After the Sermon on the Mount, Jesus says to go put it into practice. I'm a bottom-line kind of guy," says Tucker. "What's the point if we can't put it into practice?"

INTO THE WORLD

W hen she was a little girl, Susan Hellums dreamed of a life devoted to mission work. But just like most people's childhood dreams, this one was eventually overtaken by grownup sensibilities. As an adult, Hellums knew she wasn't anybody out of the ordinary— just a wife, mother of two, and church day-school director tucked away in the border town of McAllen, Texas. What made her ever think she could possibly aspire to a life that required such extraordinary gifts? She was never going to be the next Albert Schweitzer or Mother Teresa. Why, she thought, should she even try?

And then, while taking the first study in the DISCIPLE series, she was paid a visit by a couple of biblical heavyweights. The first encounter was with Jacob. Hellums closed her eyes as the story of his wrestling match with God was read during class and felt overwhelmed by emotion. "Everything kind of let loose," she recalls. "I knew that's where I was in my life."

Right on Jacob's heels was Moses, the lowly, stuttering shepherd who protested to God that he was ill-equipped to lead his people out of bondage. Once again, Hellums saw herself in the story.

"I'm no genius, I'm not particularly organized, and I'm not a good public speaker," she says. "But I saw that God will give me everything I need if I follow him. That's what it said in the Bible. . . . I know if God really wants something, he's going to lead us there, and he's going to give us all the tools we need to do it."

Soon afterward, she amazed herself when she volunteered to organize several dozen members of her church, First United Methodist of McAllen, to do repair and renovation on five houses in the town. It would be just the first step in a life now dedicated to mission.

"I think DISCIPLE made me realize that serving others is what God calls us to do as Christians," says Hellums, "and the way he was calling me to do that was through mission work. He was leading me in that direction. It just made everything come together. It gave me the courage to say 'I'll do that.' "

Though a long-term Bible study such as DISCIPLE doesn't necessarily ensure that service or mission work will follow, clearly it has proved to be a powerful motivator for a significant number of DISCIPLE graduates. Sensing God's claim on their lives can come in a flash of revelation from a single story or passage. Or it may come in a recurring whisper as the Bible is absorbed chapter by chapter. Sometimes, it comes in the form of classmates' encouragement and affirmation. But however God's claim is recognized, once it's felt, it often inspires a response to act.

"Just being in DISCIPLE and being immersed in the Bible that whole year does something to you," says John Sicher, a young father and marketing manager in Pittsburgh, Pennsylvania. "It motivates you and encourages you to do something for others, to try to live the way Jesus wants you to live, to think, 'Where can I take this and where can I take my life?' " Since completing the Bible study at his church, he has become a frequent volunteer for various projects, including organizing a holiday mission trip to a needy community in West Virginia.

Kay Weede felt "a power nudging me" during the last few DISCIPLE sessions at her Tucson, Arizona, church. "And I think that power is still nudging me. It's saying get out and share your ideas; be compassionate, caring, concerned," says the retired teacher, who has regularly volunteered at a women's shelter and for an AIDS-HIV ministry.

Lill Griffith, who works at a social service agency for underprivileged children, came to understand that God's claim goes beyond even what she had chosen for her career. "It's the willingness to serve and use our hands and feet for Christ," says the Karns City, Pennsylvania, woman who spends her free time repairing houses damaged by natural disasters or neglect. "You feel the need to make the effort, as opposed to saying, 'We ought to be doing something.' "

To Becky Scrivner, a Pensacola, Florida, homemaker who has trained her show dogs to become furry ministers at nursing homes, being faithful isn't about following a set of rules. "You have to be willing to put yourself out on a limb for Christ," she says. "You have to be willing to trust God to lead you to do something like what I'm doing now and what I'm enjoying so much. You want to grow. You want God to use you. You come out of DISCIPLE with the attitude, 'Here I am, Lord; do with me.' "

The Discovery of Gifts

When Susan Hellums took on the housing-rehab project in McAllen, Texas, she didn't really know where God was leading her, but she did know she had opened herself up to new possibilities. One arose even as she was soliciting donations for her work teams. During a conversation with a representative from a state social-service agency, she learned of a desperate need for a children's shoe bank in the area.

After the house-repair project had been successfully completed, Hellums took the idea for a shoe bank to her church, then volunteered to help put together a program. The result was a model of innovation.

Instead of matching shoes to particular children, she and the state agency devised a plan that uses vouchers. The church raises money for the vouchers through donations and grants; the state agency then administers the program through the local school system. When children enroll in classes, they're asked whether they need a new pair of shoes. If they do, they're given a voucher that's worth $15 toward discounted shoes at two local chain stores. Since the program's start in 1993, about six hundred pairs of shoes have been given away every school year, and Hellums has helped replicate the program at ten other churches in the South Texas area. Over the years, she also has continued to organize her church's annual housing-rehab projects.

These experiences only whet her appetite for more mission opportunities, and in September 2000, she finally realized her childhood dream: She accepted a full-time position as mission coordinator for her church conference. She now is in charge of coordinating the work teams and medical teams that regularly travel to the area to help the impoverished communities along the Mexican border.

"I'm having a blast. It is fun; it really is," says Hellums. "There's a lot of need, but there are so many people wanting to do good and to follow good. That's what I believe God put me here for. I'm sure there's lots of other stuff I'm not doing yet, but I'm going to try."

Over the years, Hellums has discovered gifts she didn't even know she had—something that seems to be a common occurrence among DISCIPLE graduates who have stepped out on faith. To help with the discovery process, the first study in the series actually includes an exercise in Lesson 33. During the class, the climax of the course, members are required to identify their own gifts, then talk about the gifts they perceive in one another. The results can occasionally come as a surprise.

Rusty Gordon, an Atlanta-area business executive, placed "youth work" at the bottom of his list. Every single one of his classmates, however, had ranked him Number 1 in that category. At age thirty-seven, the father of three young children thought he was too old to relate to adolescents, but his classmates had all been struck by his energy and intellectual creativity—traits they felt would be a perfect match for teens. The church's youth minister soon got wind of the class's assessment and extended an invitation for Gordon to volunteer. The Bible study, says Gordon, "gave me enough confidence . . . that I was willing to step out on faith."

The year was 1991; a decade later, Gordon had become a linchpin of the youth ministry at Roswell United Methodist Church. His activities have included teaching Sunday school and Bible studies, leading the church youth group, and taking youth to revivals, on retreats, and on tours of college campuses. He also spearheaded a successful drive to raise $3.5 million for a thirty-thousand-square-foot youth center at the church.

What Gordon worried about originally—piquing teenagers' interest, then holding their attention—has proved to be a challenge that he relishes. For one Bible study lesson, for example, he wanted to impress on his young students the sacrifice that Job's friends made when they sat silently with him for seven days. "I taught a lesson on 'What kind of friend are you?' " Gordon says. "I asked if they could sit for seven days without saying a word and just experience a friend's pain. Could they sit for seven hours? Could they sit for just seven minutes?" He then had the teens sit silently, thinking about a friend in pain, for seven minutes. "It was a lifetime!" he recalls.

Gordon never questions where he gets his ideas. "God always seems to come through," he says.

In a DISCIPLE class in Fairbanks, Alaska, Ken Krieg listened as classmates described him in terms he had never applied to himself—*prophet* and *apostle.* The next Sunday, the retired animal-science professor found a bulletin insert announcing an upcoming course to train lay speakers. "I literally didn't know what a lay speaker was," says Krieg, "but I almost could not have kept myself from signing up. It was a pretty powerful experience that told me, 'Do this,' so I did. Between that feeling and what the class said, I'd say it was abundantly clear that God had some things for me to do."

Since that day in 1997, Krieg has come to understand the course as a way to train people to find their own individual ministries. For Krieg, that meant becoming his church's "lay associate for worship and administration." In essence, he steps in when the pastor is unavailable. "It's led me to preach, witness, and teach on a regular basis," says Krieg. He's also taken it upon himself to add an extra duty to his list of responsibilities—training other lay speakers. "I felt I was being called to identify others who seemed to be ready to make a significant step forward in their spiritual lives and help them on their way," he says.

The first dozen people he's trained in the fifteen-hour course have gone on to become Sunday school teachers, substitute preachers, and church leaders; one woman has found her ministry making weekly visits to the local hospitals to chat with patients and to witness to them. "I don't consider myself a zealot or missionary or evangelist," Krieg says. "But I've also come to understand that you don't have to be a zealot or missionary or evangelist. There's lots of other ways to carry out a ministry."

When retired teacher Janice Moon went through the process of discerning her gifts with her Rockville,

Maryland, class, she thought her teaching days had passed. But her classmates had other ideas.

"They all said, 'This is your greatest talent; you should be doing this,' " says Moon. "I took it seriously. It had a great impact on me."

Within days, she ran across an article about adult illiteracy, and she suddenly got the notion to volunteer at a nearby detention center, where crime suspects are held after they're arrested and until they're either released or sentenced to prison. After taking a course on how to teach reading to adults, Moon began spending an hour twice a week with inmates. "All I require is that they know the alphabet," she says.

The circumstances that have led her students to her have never troubled Moon. "I really don't pay much attention to why they're there," she says. "I've been treated so courteously and respectfully, I'm never worried or frightened. . . . Sometimes they're the ones who are frightened. They all need assurance and a pat on the back. It's not easy if you can't read. Your life is terrible. To confront this when you're twenty, thirty, and forty takes a lot of courage."

She still doesn't know how or why she got the idea to do this volunteer work. "I guess," she says, "I have to attribute it to God."

At the Chinese United Methodist Church in New York City's Chinatown, Helen Shum discovered that using one's gifts is sometimes simply a matter of stepping up to do what needs to be done. During Lesson 33, she felt drawn to volunteer to teach a children's Sunday school class. At the time, though, the church really needed volunteers for its free legal clinic that was soon to open for United States immigrants. "I was curious and interested in what this involved, and I thought it was something that would be helpful in our community," says Shum, a native of Hong Kong who works as a management analyst for the United States Food and Drug Administration.

But what began as a small effort, almost out of a sense of

duty, soon turned into something else. A couple of months after the clinic opened in 1999, its coordinator quit unexpectedly, and Shum shocked herself by volunteering to take over. "I suppose if you had asked me before DISCIPLE if I could do what I'm doing now," she says, "I would have said no way."

Even though the clinic is open only once a month, Shum is on the telephone at least once a day, talking to clients and prospective clients. During the clinic, she works at the front desk, serving as a translator and shuttling people in to see the immigration attorney. "You feel for the clients," she says. "There are those who really couldn't afford an attorney otherwise. Some are in situations where they don't need the service as much as they need somebody to talk to—somebody who speaks their own language. Some of them don't know we're volunteers, so we explain to them this is our church and this is something we want to be involved in. . . . It's kind of strange. In the outside world, they're not used to getting something for nothing."

The work, Shum says, has given her a strong sense that she is living out her faith. "It's important to me," she says. "I don't feel like I have to be there. I want to be there."

God's Presence Revealed

When DISCIPLE graduates talk about the rewards of service, what they describe is probably typical of anyone who volunteers—making a difference, filling a vital need, connecting to others. But they also speak of something even more transcendent. Often unexpectedly, a feeling, an experience, or even just a few words can reveal God's presence in their midst.

Don Loomis, the long-time DISCIPLE leader who has taken Lill Griffith and several other graduates on work projects to areas devastated by natural disasters, remembers one trip into Kentucky in 1997 that immediately started off on the wrong foot. The volunteers, all members of Christ Community United Methodist Church in Butler, Pennsylvania, were prepared to dry-wall a flood-ravaged house. But when they arrived, they discovered it wasn't ready. The team spotted another damaged house across the street and wandered over. Inside was a young couple who had no flood insurance; they'd already stripped all the ruined dry wall, but when they were away, a thief had made off with all the exposed wiring. They didn't know what they were going to do next. The work team immediately shifted gears.

"By the end of the week, we rewired their place, insulated it, dry-walled it, spackled it, and had the first coat painted," says Loomis. "The couple was flabbergasted. They were just speechless. They'd had no expectation for any help."

The couple didn't attend a church, so at week's end, the team presented them with a Bible and told them about a nearby Methodist church. "Six months later, we got a letter from the woman that said she was going to church," Loomis recalls. "Six months after that, she wrote to say her husband, her mother, and her grandmother were all going regularly. We figured it wasn't only a mission trip to repair a home but to get some people into a spiritual life. That was a great feeling."

John Sicher found new meaning in Christmas by helping to organize a holiday mission trip in 2000 for members at Ingomar United Methodist Church in Pittsburgh. The church had done summer mission work in the West Virginia town of Philippi—a poor community with the same name as the one the Apostle Paul visited—but Sicher wanted to cinch the ties with a Christmas dinner and gift-giving. Invitations went out to all the people who'd been helped in the summer, and they filled out and returned Christmas wish lists. Everyone gathered together at a Philippi church.

"There were about fifty of us and about seventy-five of them," recalls the marketing manager. "I was waiting on people, passing out dessert. There was one woman who'd finished her dinner, and I was going to take her paper plate and give her a new plate. But she stopped me."

"No, put it here," she said, pointing to her dinner plate. It was wasteful, she explained, to use a new one.

"A paper plate!" Sicher exclaims, savoring the moment. "When has it crossed my mind not to be wasteful about a paper plate?" It was an experience, he says, "that really put things in perspective for me. . . . It made my Christmas a lot more special."

For Becky Scrivner, there are small miracles awaiting each Thursday afternoon when she brings one of her two trained Australian shepherds, Flint and Koty, to a Pensacola, Florida, assisted-living residence for the elderly. "Every time I go, there are usually eight or so folks waiting for us in the lobby, sitting there patiently. Sometimes they're standing at the door," says Scrivner. "I'll let them love on Flint or Koty; then we move to the different chairs and couches." After that, she and her dog make the rounds to the various rooms. "There's one little lady, every time I go in, her face is so gloomy, but she's a whole different person when we leave. I think that's how I'll be in a nursing home. I hope somebody brings me a dog."

When Scrivner and her shepherd are ready to leave, one elderly woman insists on walking them to the car. She's so frail that, once the dog is in the car, Scrivner then insists on walking her back to the residence door. "She stands under the carport, and I roll my window down," says Scrivner, "and she waves to me the whole time I'm leaving."

Scrivner says she can tell that Flint and Koty enjoy the visits as much as she and the residents do. "They are so good," she says. "It's like God created them to do that. They know how much love they're expressing."

Though countless DISCIPLE graduates have frequently

found these kinds of unexpected returns for their generosity, there's never a guarantee that a positive outcome lies ahead. Lill Griffith has felt the pleasure of putting people back on their feet when she repairs homes in disaster-stricken areas, but her experience has often been far different working on neglected houses in her Pennsylvania hometown. "Traditionally, in families with abuse and neglect, the norm is they'll go back to the way they were living," she says. "Interestingly, the very first house we worked on, I recently heard the news that she's living in filth again."

Griffith, though, doesn't regret her effort. "Our call is, we saw a need and went and did it," she says. "If we judged everything we did in terms of the gratitude we get, we might not be doing it."

Anyway, she says, serving others really isn't about getting results: It's about "what God wants us to be out and about and doing."

CHAPTER SIX

CHURCH CONVERSIONS

The folks who showed up for service that Sunday morning at East Longmeadow United Methodist Church won't forget the sight any time soon. Wrapped around the entire church were yards upon yards of yellow construction-site tape that warned "CAUTION." Once the mystified churchgoers stepped over and under it, they found even more yellow tape inside, draping the front of the sanctuary.

What was going on here—a surprise building campaign?

Janet Smith-Rushton, pastor of the church in the small south-central Massachusetts town of East Longmeadow, ended the suspense with her announcement: Registration for the next round of DISCIPLE Bible study classes was about to begin. And this time, she added, members needed to exercise caution. "Sign up," she said, "only if you're willing to be changed."

After just one round of DISCIPLE classes, Smith-Rushton had discovered the Bible study's transformative effect on this once sluggish congregation. Fifty of the church's 125 adult regulars had taken DISCIPLE during that previous school year, 1995–96, and a new spirit seemed to be pulsing through the church. She could feel it, and she could see it. People were stepping up and volunteering to teach Sunday school and get trained for youth work—no arm-twisting required. The collection plates were coming back laden with new generosity. Church-meeting discussions were featuring a new topic—outreach ministry.

"It was the transformational power that got let loose," says Smith-Rushton. "That's the difference between simply being a church and being alive. Once I felt that vitality unleashed, I knew I didn't ever want to do anything else. I didn't want people to settle for less. . . . It's too exciting to settle for less."

Across the country, congregations—small and large, in cities and towns—have embraced the Bible study not just as a spiritual source for individual members but also as a change agent for the church. Pastors, often with equal measures of hope and trepidation, have taken up DISCIPLE as a tool to address whatever pressing challenge was at hand. Unfortunately, it is the familiar list of woes facing churches today—spiritual stagnation, dwindling numbers, social insulation and apathy, even wrenching scandal.

Every church has its own personality, customs, and issues; and so naturally, a Bible study will work in each church in different ways. Certainly not every congregation where DISCIPLE is offered has experienced a transformation as palpable as East Longmeadow's; pastors and parishioners at many churches describe DISCIPLE as a modest program that simply fills the steady need for Bible study.

Why would some congregations be more transformed by DISCIPLE than others? For a number of reasons, but key among them appears to be the level of a pastor's support and participation. It's not enough for ministers to endorse lay or staff efforts to launch a Bible study. In the spectacularly successful programs, preachers promote DISCIPLE from the pulpit, extend personal invitations to members, and often lead the classes themselves. It can be an enormous investment of energy and time, but the pastors who do it say the dividends reaped by their congregations are incalculable.

Stirring Up a Revival

Bible study, says Robert Schnase, has always been the "cornerstone" of his ministry. No wonder, when he arrived in McAllen, Texas, in 1989 to pastor a downtown church, that one of his first steps was to start DISCIPLE classes. "It seems like Bible study comes first," says Schnase, "and everything is going to flow from it. . . . It not only enriches spiritual life, but it also gives you a way to make contact with the congregation at a much deeper level."

In 1989 First United Methodist of McAllen was a church in decline. Fewer than two hundred people were worshiping on Sundays; morale was low, and the stately brick structure was mostly empty during the week. Schnase got to work and announced he would be leading a long-term Bible study; he was delighted when thirty-seven people signed up. "I had one class of nineteen and another of eighteen, and I taught two evenings a week." The participants turned out to be the core that would reignite the church. "I look at that first group of thirty-seven," Schnase says, "and at the opportunity I had as a new pastor to have that quality of interaction on a whole range of issues, . . . and I think it changed the direction of the congregation."

Out of the first two classes, new leaders stepped forward; new ideas for ministry bubbled to the surface. In the next three years, four church members took DISCIPLE leadership training, and 180 more people completed the first study in the series; many continued with subsequent studies. The congregation was deepening; it also was growing. By 2000 the church boasted a membership of one thousand, and adults in their thirties and forties proved to be the fastest growing segment. In September of that year, ground was broken on the first phase of a $5 million complex a few miles away.

Since the move to new quarters in May 2002, the congregation has been able to expand the activities that already teemed in the original structure—fellowship events, mission projects, an assortment of Bible studies, a Christian preschool.

DISCIPLE Bible study isn't the only reason for the congregation's transformation, says Schnase, but "it was at the center of moving us forward." It also has been crucial in the congregation's understanding of one of the most important, and prickly, issues in any church—stewardship.

Traditionally, Schnase explains, stewardship is "constantly focused on financial numbers and the need of the church to receive. I think that's got it all backwards. [It's] about Christians' need to give; it's about developing our relationship with God and our relationship with other people—to see our lives in terms of what we contribute. There's just so far we can go with our spiritual growth until we can confront the money monster face to face and say, 'You're not going to win. I'm in control of my worldly possessions in a way that serves God.' That kind of discussion required a real change in how we looked at all the financial issues—and that discussion took place multiple times in Bible studies. . . . We hit that theme and backed off, hit it and backed off, and it just kind of ripened until we could talk seriously about how we do finances in the church."

Now when there's a call for pledges "it is not to meet a financial goal," the pastor says. "It's to meet a spiritual goal." Consequently, no target amount is set; church officers count the money as it comes. And it has come in abundance. By the time construction on the new church began, the congregation had raised $2.6 million—four times the church's annual $650,000 budget. An average campaign raises 2.7 times an annual budget.

A Sense of Mission

When pastor Diana Facemyer arrived at tiny St. Thomas United Methodist Church in Glen Ellyn, Illinois, in 1995, she discovered a congregation aimlessly coasting. The church had been the last stop before retirement for its previous two pastors; longtime member Dave Thorpe describes it as less a church than "a friendly club."

In Facemyer's first few days, a church member suggested a "comprehensive Bible study." The ebullient pastor had heard the magic words. Bible study had long been her passion, and she had taught DISCIPLE at her previous congregation.

But Facemyer saw the study as more than a chance to acquaint herself with her congregation, and her congregation with the Bible. She was determined to use it as a way for the church to chart its course in ministry. "I believe," says Facemyer, "that when people understand who they are and how loved they are by God, something grows in them that must respond to that. That's what I love about it. I love that I can't predict it and I can't control it. I just sit back and watch it happen in the lives of people."

What happened in that first class—after thirty-four weeks of discussion, daily study, and prayer—was a strong call to mission work. "I learned so much from the Bible," says Thorpe, who joined the church in 1980. "It teaches you that you have to get out and nurture the world. You don't keep it inside." Granted, outreach is the sort of ministry tackled more handily by larger churches—not one with only about one hundred regular members. But if these members wanted to do mission work, the pastor wasn't about to let their wishes go unfulfilled.

Soon the middle-class suburban congregation was identifying itself as "a mission-centered church." In Facemyer's first seven years at St. Thomas, mission teams ranging from a dozen to twenty people traveled to Ohio, South Dakota, and Appalachia. They worked on blood drives and charity races. Every other month, members took a fourteen-hour night shift at a homeless shelter. And in April 2001, the church sent a work team of twenty to Honduras.

Participants in the mission trips always do a presentation at a Sunday service after their return, "and we always have people say, 'I'm going next time,'" says Thorpe's wife, Norma, a retired federal worker who's the church's part-time secretary. "Some have had DISCIPLE, and some haven't, but I think DISCIPLE is part of the spark, because the people who've taken it are so enthusiastic."

After four rounds of classes, forty people have graduated from at least the first study in the DISCIPLE series. Facemyer knows these members are the ones she can always count on to volunteer for church leadership, to teach Sunday school, to suggest new mission possibilities. "With forty disciples," she says, "that's a percolating caldron of faith."

Wounds Inflicted, Then Healed

A beloved church worker is accused of a crime, and the news rocks the congregation. Members choose sides, and the church starts to tear apart at the seams. Incidents like this have irreparably crippled and even extinguished churches, but not in this case. This time, the presence of two ongoing Bible studies acted as a healing force during a congregation's most troubled hour.

Even though the church where this particular event occurred is now trying to put the past to rest, many of the people involved in the painful episode still value its lessons. And so they have shared their story on the condition that their names and the church's location be omitted and some identifying details be changed.

The incident began in May 1994 with the sharing of a secret. A fourteen-year-old youth came to his pastor and confided he had been molested by the church's longtime youth director. Believing the boy was telling the truth, the pastor persuaded him that steps had to be taken. The boy's parents were told. Law officials were summoned; an investigation was begun. But when news spread through the three-hundred-member congregation, allegiances quickly formed around the popular worker. The boy's family became frightened, and just as quickly, they withdrew their cooperation. The case was dropped, but the episode was hardly over. Making confidential inquiries, the staff-parish committee concluded the youth director might have been involved in other incidents. The panel also learned that, if another youth stepped forward with a similar accusation, a strong suit could be brought against the church as long as the worker was still on staff. An agonizing decision was made to fire the man. Immediately, cries of protest went up. "They needed somebody to blame," says the pastor, "and they blamed me."

Gossip and innuendo swirled. The pastor received anonymous threats, and his tires were slashed. Church members who had been friends for years suddenly were no longer speaking to one another.

And through it all, two DISCIPLE classes, both led by the pastor, kept meeting week after week at the church. Somehow, every class kept to the week's lesson; and somehow, every lesson seemed to relate to what was happening in the church.

There was the wisdom of the ridiculed prophets, and the people's struggle over who was their enemy and who was their brother; there was Paul's firm counsel to the unruly congregation in Corinth. Then came the questions posed to the class members: "How is your church being faithful in the midst of crisis?" "Who are today's martyrs?" "How do some attitudes get in the way of witness?" In one lesson, the study manual suggested students write letters of reconciliation. Several took the task to heart, and they actually mailed what they'd written to angry parishioners. "They were asking for peace; they were asking for understanding;

they were asking for harmony," the pastor recalls. Each week, the classes always ended with prayer concerns. Always, there was prayer for the church.

Within the constructive context of Bible study, "DISCIPLE allowed the dialogue to happen," says one class member, a schoolteacher. Not everyone agreed on the action taken against the youth director, but "we were still able to share in a positive way," says another member, a legal secretary. "We were all searching for some meaning out of it, for some salvation for our congregation."

In face-to-face dealings with other parishioners, the students had bountiful opportunity to live out their lessons. "I think the DISCIPLE group and those who were being affected by that group really were the people showing integrity and showing how to stand up under adversity without playing dirty," says the teacher. They were the ones who worked to keep folks coming to church, who worked to make sure the church's commitments to a local charity were fulfilled. "We felt it was important to keep things going," the secretary says.

But still, by March 1995, the congregation remained in the grip of the conflict. During one class, the pastor recalls, "I remember their saying, 'What can we do? What did Paul do?' " Out of that discussion, someone suggested a mediator. The idea of bringing in an outsider had crossed the pastor's mind, but he says, "I had not progressed to a point of doing anything about it. I needed to hear from them the consensus—to confirm to me that the Spirit was at work."

In a series of congregational meetings, the mediator was able to temper emotions and to open lines of communication. With tensions easing, DISCIPLE participants stepped forward to "develop new programs, get involved in new projects, and get people back into Sunday school," says the teacher.

The conversations continued over the next year as two more DISCIPLE classes formed. But these offered a time for more than healing. During the course of study, two class members came to the pastor with a horrible confession. They had gone on youth trips with the fired staffer; they had seen him act inappropriately with other boys. "We knew what was going on," one said, "and we turned our heads." For them DISCIPLE offered a time for repentance.

When the Ground Shifts

Any church that attempts to launch a full-scale DISCIPLE program has no way of predicting exactly where it will lead, or even if it will kindle a communal transformation. On top of that, with its daily readings and weekly classes, DISCIPLE requires heavy commitment; many pastors contemplating ways to enlist a congregation can practically hear the congregation groan. Convincing a church to take part in the program and then maintaining enthusiasm for it have to take patient commitment, thoughtful planning, and more than a little creativity.

No one proved the importance of patience better than Janet Smith-Rushton, the pastor of the tiny Massachusetts church. She had been at East Longmeadow United Methodist for four years when the congregation began talking in vague terms of a spiritual hunger in 1993. "I knew intuitively that people did yearn to know the Word of God," she says, "yet Bible study in the local church had not been a core value." She invited a Methodist conference representative to talk about DISCIPLE to the church council. The church leaders' reaction was unanimous, she recalls. "They said it's a great program—and no one will ever do it. I was just deflated." But she wasn't defeated. After the meeting, two members quietly came up and told her they would take DISCIPLE if it were offered. "I knew people would respond," she says, "but we needed more time. So we waited."

About six months later, members of the church's visioning committee suggested Smith-Rushton invite laypeople from another church to tell about their DISCIPLE experience. And so she did. "I remember it as being one of the most electric, energetic meetings we'd ever had," she says. "The committee really caught the spirit, and at the end, they said, 'What a great program. We'll have to do it . . . someday.'" Smith-Rushton mustered more patience; she could tell the ground had shifted a bit.

In fact, after another six months, the church council finally agreed to send the pastor and the youth director to DISCIPLE training. It was a crucial step, Smith-Rushton knew, but yet to come was the greatest one of all—recruiting a class. Something her DISCIPLE trainer said stuck with her, though: "You have to believe that people want to be transformed by the Word." Hearing that, she realized, "That's what's missing in my ministry. I haven't leaned into believing people yearn for the Word of God."

For the next three months, she preached about DISCIPLE. She kept bringing it up in conversation. She extended personal invitations to sign up. And she led the congregation in prayer; all they prayed for was twelve—just twelve people to start one class. One Sunday she put a DISCIPLE graduate in the pulpit to tell her story, and afterward, Smith-Rushton heard the sanctuary murmurs, "Are you going to do it?" "If you do it, I'll do it."

When she checked the sign-up sheets, she found fifty names—more than a quarter of the regular members and enough for three adult classes and one youth class. "I didn't have the heart to tell a whole class to wait," she says, "so I did three classes." It had taken her fifteen months to get a program up and running, but "that next year, DISCIPLE was the whole focus of our church."

At his Atlanta church, pastor Rodney Smothers relied on a little righteous subterfuge to get the new volunteer director of education into DISCIPLE training in 1990. Annette Bond was an old friend who implicitly trusted her pastor, so she didn't think twice when she agreed to attend "a training conference for church leaders." Little did she know it would be preparing her to lead a thirty-four-week Bible study. "He knew I had such a weird schedule," says Bond, who was in sales management at the time, "and I would probably have said, 'Oh, I don't have time to do that.' But I went and took the training, and I got totally charged."

Smothers had recently been appointed to Central United Methodist, a once-vital church in the inner city that was in such decline, he says wryly, "that one church member told me, 'You could throw a dead body on Sunday morning and when it landed, it wouldn't hit anybody.' " Together, he and Bond masterminded a DISCIPLE ministry that resurrected the congregation over the next few years. The program revolved around a Wednesday night jam-packed with activities for the whole family: DISCIPLE classes, short-term Bible study, and other enrichment courses for adults; DISCIPLE classes for youth; Bible classes for younger children. The evening kicked off at 6:00 P.M. with a sit-down supper that diners paid for; it was prepared by the church's "cooking ministry"—women in the church who loved working in the kitchen. A "parking ministry" was organized to greet visitors in the parking lot, to watch over the cars, and to offer escorts at the end of the evening. "Some of the wives were saying, 'To have my husband here with my children, and we're all here doing something—it's a dream we've all had,' " says Bond. "We had people driving thirty and forty miles just to come." Within a couple of years, the church was averaging 250 people on Wednesday nights. Sunday morning worship attendance eventually revived to average around nine hundred at two services.

Even though there were educational offerings for adults besides DISCIPLE, "everything revolved around it," says Bond. "We had DISCIPLE banners all around, and people wore their DISCIPLE pins." Participants in the short-term Bible studies usually committed to the longer study, she says, "once they got in the habit of coming on Wednesday night and finding out it wasn't so bad." Start-ups of new classes were staggered throughout the year, so persons expressing an interest in taking DISCIPLE could be quickly obliged.

In 1998 Bond ended up following Smothers to help him at his next charge, a struggling church in Lithonia, an Atlanta suburb. Once again, they successfully launched a Wednesday night curriculum. To Smothers, the midweek event "is the missing link [in ministry]. Churches grow, but they don't grow to the next level without that link that prepares people for leadership and service. That's what forces them to think deeply about their relationship with Jesus Christ, and in light of this: Where does God want me to serve? What does God want me to do? How can I live out the call upon my life?"

Huge Churches, Huge Triumphs

Maintaining and promoting a DISCIPLE program has become a science, if not an art, at two "megachurches"— one in an Atlanta suburb, the other in a Kansas City suburb. In fact, both have come to rely on their programs to address the challenges that face larger congregations, but each has tailored its program in markedly different ways.

Roswell United Methodist Church began its first DISCIPLE class in 1989, when its congregation already numbered more than five thousand. Since then, the Bible study has gradually become almost a rite of passage at the church. Sally Dowland, the director of adult ministries, remembers noticing the cultural shift in the mid-1990s when members started talking about "when," not "if," they would take DISCIPLE.

Still, the church, located north of Atlanta in the city of Roswell, has been measured and methodical in its approach; in fourteen years, only about twelve hundred members have completed at least the first study in the series. That figure is just 16 percent of its 7,600 membership. "We've grown it each year, but not rapidly, which is different from other large congregations," Dowland explains. The reason, she says, is the church's commitment to a certain quality of class experience. "We're very picky about the leaders," she says. "Not just any warm body can sign up. We've been very careful in gift discernment. There is a special gift in DISCIPLE leadership, so we don't assume everyone who's taken it is going to be a great leader."

With little exception, DISCIPLE students at Roswell qualify to lead only if they are invited by their own class leaders; also, most of the dozen or so classes each year are co-led. As a result, she says, there often are not enough leaders to meet demand—something that was perceived as a problem at first but is now considered an asset. "It still kills me after twelve years of doing this to tell someone there's no room," says Dowland, who has been a Roswell member for fifteen years. "Yet it's made the point that, hey, lots of people want to do this. Next year, they're a lot quicker to sign up."

Word of mouth provides most of the promotion that the Bible study needs, but the church has also developed an introductory session conducted in Sunday school classes on request. DISCIPLE leaders come in with study manuals and a video, and they lead the class in an abbreviated lesson.

The church also has started a regular event called a "DISCIPLE World Dinner." Scheduled about once a year, it's targeted to "any DISCIPLE graduate, any current participant, and anyone who's interested in DISCIPLE," says Dowland— which, she adds, of course means everybody. Many DISCIPLE graduates have used it as an opportunity for a class reunion. Held in the church's fellowship hall, the dinner is a fancy affair with tablecloths and candlelight, elaborate centerpieces, and live dinner music. The three to four hundred guests each pay $10 for an elegant meal catered by the church's kitchen staff. The keynote speaker is a Disciple notable, such as study coauthor Richard Wilke or J. Ellsworth Kalas, an author and professor of homiletics who appears in the videos. The event is primarily a time for celebration, says Dowland, but it also has proved to be a recruiting tool.

In Leawood, Kansas, the United Methodist Church of the Resurrection has put its Disciple program on a fast track. But then, when a congregation grows to six thousand members only a decade after its birth, just about everything is on a fast track.

The church, southwest of Kansas City, was founded by a dynamic twenty-six-year-old preacher named Adam Hamilton in 1990. About three years later, he recruited Dave Robertson, then twenty-nine, to be the congregation's director of discipleship and to help him achieve the church's purpose—"to build a community where the non-religious and the nominally religious are becoming deeply committed Christians."

"How do we become deeply committed Christians?" Robertson asks, then answers, "Disciple is the way to start. . . . But once you get into it, it's not the end of it. It's the foundation."

Robertson was previously a director of youth ministry and evangelism at a church in McKinney, Texas, just north of Dallas. It was there that he first led a Disciple class and as he puts it, "I found my calling." During Robertson's first six years at Church of the Resurrection, eleven hundred members graduated from the Disciple program he put in place. Then in a major promotional push in 2000, the church enrolled one thousand students in fifty-six Disciple classes. "We've always set very high goals," says Robertson, "and God has always matched them."

Churchgoers are likely to first learn about Disciple during "Coffee With the Pastor," a regular event for people inquiring about membership. After Hamilton has told them that members are expected to do something outside of weekly worship to "grow in their faith," Robertson follows up with his introduction to DISCIPLE. Once churchgoers plug into a group—whether it's a weekly Sunday school class, a four-week study of a Gospel, or a ten-week Alpha course, the goal is still to nudge them toward DISCIPLE. Just to make sure they get the message, Robertson has produced a video addressing the excuses most commonly used to put off DISCIPLE, such as "My spouse doesn't want to take it with me" or "I don't want to walk into a class of strangers."

Every year, a bulk mailing goes out to everyone who has ever attended the church—eleven thousand by 2000— inviting them to join a DISCIPLE class. The mail includes not only an enrollment form but also a list of every DISCIPLE graduate in the church. "That's to say 'Find someone and call them,'" says Robertson. "We want everyone to be a living testimony."

People can enroll by mail or telephone (the church has a designated "DISCIPLE hot line"), or they can simply stop Robertson in a church hallway; he'll be happy to fill out one of the enrollment forms he carries with him. Obviously here is someone who's hard to turn down, although one man did try once. He told Robertson his job as a business executive required him to work long hours; he had six kids; he just didn't have the time. Surely, Robertson said, he had a couple of free hours—any hours—during the week. The man thought for a minute. Well, maybe he did have a couple of hours. And that is how Robertson found himself leading a weekly DISCIPLE class at lunchtime in a corporate office complex.

CHAPTER SEVEN

A SHEPHERD AND HIS FLOCK

Zan W. Holmes, Jr., knew he was little more than a face in the crowd at the Houston awards event in June 1997. To be sure, he was among the dozen or so Texans being honored for their work in state politics. But the United Methodist minister from Dallas was sharing the bill with celebrated men and women who had once been Texas governors, United States senators and representatives, even a presidential cabinet member.

Seated next to him at his table was the vice president of the United States, Al Gore, and Ann Richards, the flamboyant former governor. Holmes acted the spectator as guests thronged to shake hands with the two political superstars. When one woman approached with her camera, the pastor obligingly rose to remove himself from the picture.

"No, no!" the woman blurted out. "I don't want them! I want you!"

Holmes looked at her in bewilderment.

"I'm in DISCIPLE!" she said.

Suddenly and mysteriously upstaged, Richards turned to Holmes. "What's DISCIPLE?"

At this point in telling the story, Holmes has to stop, no longer able to suppress his infectious laugh. It rattles and rolls like a jazz drum solo.

"And she had her husband take the picture," he says, the laughter subsiding to a chuckle. "Gore and Ann Richards, they were just sitting there watching, like, 'What is this?' . . . I mean, it's just wild. It's wild."

There's the Man!

When he agreed in 1987 to present the introductions on all thirty-four videos that accompany the first study in the DISCIPLE series, Holmes really had no idea what he was getting himself into. But now he knows. For the hundreds of thousands of DISCIPLE graduates, Zan Holmes has come to almost personify the Bible study.

Over the course of the study, as weeks turn into months, students begin to feel as if they know this eloquent preacher with the friendly face and resonant voice. One New England pastor recounts how quickly the boys in her youth DISCIPLE class connected with Holmes. "There's the man!" they called out when he appeared on screen during the early weeks of the study. In the final weeks, she said, the call had changed: "There's my man!"

His active speaking schedule is, more often than not, due to his role in DISCIPLE. Rarely a week passes without at least one invitation arriving from a church involved in the study. Wherever he goes—airports, hotel lobbies, meeting rooms—he has grown used to the requests to shake his hand, to autograph study manuals, to hear DISCIPLE stories.

Holmes remains in awe of the impression he's made; but with typical humility, he gives himself little of the credit.

"They see me every week, and it's like I'm their companion, their friend," he says, reflecting in his cluttered pastor's study just a few months before his retirement in 2002. "But it's deeper than that. That Bible study just makes such a big difference." He understands that difference better than most; in the congregation he led for twenty-eight years, DISCIPLE has come to be the foundation of ministry.

The church, St. Luke Community United Methodist, is considered among the most prominent African-American "megachurches" in the country. At any given time, program coordinators estimate, about half the five thousand members—predominantly professional, mobile, and middle class—have completed at least the first study in the DISCIPLE series. Every year, anywhere from 350 to 550 adults and youth are taking a course.

The impact of Bible study, and the concept of discipleship, reverberates in almost every aspect of church life: from the worship services to the business meetings, from the youth ministry to the mission outreach, from the new membership to the leadership. It's made its mark even in the way the sanctuary is decorated.

Stepping inside the semicircular space—a surprisingly intimate room though it seats twelve hundred—Holmes proudly points to the two colorful banners that flank the choir loft. He reads aloud the first banner: "Jesus saves and liberates us." And then the second: "For discipleship in the community."

"That's our mission statement," he says. "So the word *discipleship* is central."

If you know who you are, Holmes believes, it's important to proclaim it in big, bold letters. And clearly, the people of St. Luke know who they are; they know what they have been called by God to do. For this group of Christians, the empty cross is more than a symbol of Jesus' triumph. The vertical beam signifies humankind's call to connect with God; the horizontal beam stands for people's connection to one another—for the call to community life. For this reason,

Holmes refers to St. Luke as "a cross-shaped church."

No road-to-Damascus moment brought this church to such a strong sense of self-identity. It is the product of a lengthy evolution and years of struggle—struggle that became fruitful, Holmes says, only after the congregation turned to Bible study.

Allowing the Bible to Speak

When he first arrived at the church in 1974 at age thirty-nine, it was hunkered down in a survival mode with about fifty members. Over the next decade, he set about to build a congregation in the spirit of community activism, and the congregation mobilized over an assortment of civic, political, and social issues. Membership steadily climbed toward a thousand; its profile in Dallas, too, was on the rise. But Holmes still felt something was lacking in the church. Despite their fervor, members didn't seem to perceive their activism as an expression of their Christian purpose; they simply didn't know enough about the Bible to see the relationship. "The sense of community was there," he says, "but the grounding was not."

Yes, he was preaching from the Bible, but few church members were coming to the Word on their own. He discovered many members didn't even own Bibles. He also noticed another disturbing development: Several in the congregation were leaving for "Bible churches." Simply because preachers held a Bible in their hands as they delivered their sermons, says Holmes, these congregants felt they were getting more from Scripture. One day, Holmes decided, "I wasn't going to let anybody out-Bible me."

From his own personal history, he knew grasping Scripture requires a purposeful approach. Though raised in the church—the son of a Methodist pastor in Waco, Texas—Holmes says he didn't feel he had truly encountered the Bible until several years after he'd finished seminary and started his own ministry in Dallas in the late 1950s.

"It came at a point of crisis in my life," he says. "I began to experience some burnout. I did not know what was wrong. I was preaching and I wasn't connecting, and I struggled. It was a struggle of the soul. And what I discovered in that time was that I was not nourishing my spiritual life. That is, I was reading the Bible, but I was not reading the Bible devotionally. Every time I picked up the Bible, I was treating it as a tool. I was looking for sermons, but I was not allowing the Bible to speak to me. . . . And that really became the turning point."

From that moment on, he began his Bible study with prayer. Then, as he read, he began to ask questions. How did the text intersect with his life and with his soul? What was God saying specifically to him? Once he discerned that, he found he was bringing the Word to others in a way he never could before.

But by the mid-1980s, he came to yet another realization. It wasn't enough that he was preaching from his own understanding of the Bible. His congregation needed to know the Scriptures for themselves.

Several immediate steps were taken at St. Luke. The church began to sell Bibles, at cost, every Sunday. Members also were required to bring their Bibles to church. Holmes instituted a regular "Bible check," asking the people in the pews to hold up their Bibles.

Holmes and worship planners also decided that he would start preaching from the lectionary and that weekly Bible studies would focus on that Scripture. Dick Murray, the Christian education expert who went on to play a key role in DISCIPLE's development, led training sessions for Bible study leaders; and within a couple of years, about thirty in-home study groups had formed. Holmes began to feel the congregation was on the right track.

"From the feedback I got, I felt it was like we were a team working together in the worship experience," he says.

A Class Becomes a Family

Yet despite the success, by the late 1980s, Holmes and others in the church were sensing the lectionary studies were running their course. No one was getting a complete picture of Scripture; people were learning the Bible in dribs and drabs. "I think you felt better prepared for Sunday," says long-time church member Shirley Ison-Newsome, "but still there was a yearning for more."

She and others also recall how the sessions often tended to go astray, turning into discussions over church or community issues and sometimes merely into social hours; attendance, as well, was spotty. At the same time, new stresses were developing. The congregation was growing by phenomenal leaps and bounds; between 1988 and 1993, two thousand members joined the church. The old sanctuary, which seated about four hundred, was being strained beyond capacity and had to be replaced. Holmes, too, was being pulled in a thousand different ways. He not only was a professor of Perkins School of Theology at Southern Methodist University, but he also was now one of the leading voices of social justice in a city riven by racial differences.

Given Holmes's prominent role in DISCIPLE, one would assume St. Luke was among the first churches to plunge into the study. Indeed, Holmes says, his work on the videos convinced him early on of DISCIPLE's transformative potential. Yet the first class didn't form at St. Luke until three years after the study's introduction.

If there is a reason for the lag, Holmes says, it is simply that he was stretched too thin; he couldn't find the time to take the training, let alone lead a class. Finally, in 1989, when Harry Wright arrived as the church's first full-time associate pastor, someone was on board who could set a program in motion.

"He just invited me to take this on, and then he got out

of the way to let me do it," recalls Wright, now the chaplain at an Asheville, North Carolina, private school. A few months later, he attended a training event in Houston, and "it was such a powerful experience that I'll never forget it."

In the summer of 1990, Holmes promoted the upcoming class from the pulpit, and Wright worked to recruit church members who already were serving in leadership positions. Both men met with the typical resistance. Cynthia Ratcliff, a mother of three and one of the most active members in the church, well remembers those first announcements. "I heard 'thirty-four weeks,' " she says. "I thought, no way!"

Eventually, twelve parishioners signed up, and the sessions began in a church meeting room. The first few weeks, Wright recalls, became a time for people who had worshiped together for years to finally get acquainted. "It's funny how you can be in the same congregation, but we didn't know each other," says Wright. "We didn't know each other's kids or what was going on in each other's lives."

But as discussion about each lesson flowed, one by one the students started talking about the Scripture in terms of their own lives. "Each week the comfort level grew as one person would share, then the next person," Wright says. "By the middle of it, people would talk about their divorce or about abuse . . . Often, we'd be in the midst of discussion and people would be brought to tears."

To Wright, the beauty of DISCIPLE is the way it can work on participants in three ways: the daily diet of the Word, the structured discipline of the weekly class, and the group-bonding experience. During one of the early meetings, students decided to pass around a calendar and divide duties, so a potluck supper would be waiting for them every week. "When we'd finish our lesson, we'd go in and grab a paper plate and eat," Wright recalls. "So it really made it a fellowship time."

Soon Holmes was witnessing the effect of DISCIPLE. After

church service, members of the class were coming up to him with questions and comments about his sermons that told him they had been doing their studies. "I knew something was happening in that group," Holmes says. "I saw people in that first group become active, more involved in the church in other ways. I could see something was happening even in Harry himself."

As the months passed, the group "became a family, in the best possible understanding," says Martin McLee, a class member who is now a minister in Boston, Massachusetts. "We looked out for each other. We prayed for one another's needs and concerns. . . . There were tremendous breakthroughs in the class—lots of 'lights going on' moments."

One of the women in the class was two months pregnant when the study started. As she neared her delivery date, she was ordered to have bed rest, and she no longer could leave her home. So the class came to her. "That brought another level of intimacy," McLee recalls, "and the dialogue took on a different complexion."

Eventually she gave birth to a healthy boy, and "it's like we all had a baby—it was a DISCIPLE baby!" Wright says. "When it came time for the baby to be christened, everyone in the group was up there. We just felt we all had a part."

For graduation, Holmes invited the class to stand before the congregation, and he asked members to share some of their experiences. "Of course, a couple of people would start talking and they'd start crying," Wright says, "and everyone would choke up."

Cynthia Ratcliff, the one who had instantly dismissed a thirty-four-week study the year before, was so moved by the testimonies that she signed up that day to take the next class. Raised in the Roman Catholic Church, she had never studied the Bible, and she suddenly realized just how much she longed for it. Many others signed up that day too, and—as Wright puts it—"that was the beginning of the igniting of the flame."

Being Fruitful and Multiplying

Seeing where the church's DISCIPLE program is today, one can't help but be reminded of how another ministry two thousand years ago started with a mere twelve people. Out of those first dozen DISCIPLE students at St. Luke, three took the training, and they, along with Wright, went on to facilitate four classes the next year. (At St. Luke, the preferred terminology is *facilitate* and *facilitator*.) From those classes, more potential facilitators were identified, and more classes formed. And still the program kept growing. "When we moved beyond that first group to the other groups, it was just magnetic," says Holmes.

Every year now, thirty or more DISCIPLE classes are organized; anywhere from two to six classes meet at the church five days out of the week. Keeping the level of participation strong and enthusiasm high takes detailed planning. The entire program follows a set calendar that begins with a full month of promotion. At each of the two Sunday services during all of July, a different DISCIPLE graduate comes forward to give his or her testimony. Those moved to sign up can find forms in their bulletins or in the church foyer; and if they forget to turn them in, they can just phone in their registrations to the church.

Classes run through fall, winter, and spring. A one-hour orientation is always held on the last Sunday afternoon in August, and during his tenure, Holmes was always there to offer a personal welcome. His successor, Tyrone D. Gordon, has continued the tradition.

Graduation—held during worship services on the last Sunday in June—has become a much-anticipated celebration at the church. The women graduates all dress in white, and the men wear their finest suits; the DISCIPLE alumni proudly don their pins. "We call them our two-, three-, and four-star generals," says Arthur Gregg, a member who has facilitated four classes.

With so many graduates to recognize, the classes are split between the two services. At the appointed moment, the DISCIPLE coordinator takes the microphone and calls out the list of names. The applause swells and the tears flow as the graduates walk down the aisles to receive their certificates and pins. Then all previous DISCIPLE graduates are invited to stand. When the masses rise, the sanctuary "just erupts," says Gregg, a university administrator. "It's like being in Texas Stadium and Dallas scores the winning touchdown at the last second of the game."

DISCIPLE facilitators at St. Luke enjoy developing their own individual styles, which often keep their students coming back for more. Two of the most requested facilitators are accomplished professional educators. Shirley Ison-Newsome, an area superintendent for the Dallas school district, is a beloved taskmaster who relies on an overhead projector and stacks of transparencies in her class discussions, and she rewards her students with star stickers for good work: red for answering questions in the study manual, green for class participation, gold for extra credit, and always a silver "because we love each other." The stars, she says with no small amusement, are a "big deal for these adults. It's amazing." Another popular facilitator is Thomas Spann, associate director of the intern program at Perkins School of Theology who holds a doctorate in ministry; he leads intense discussions in his DISCIPLE classes on the African influences in the Bible, as well as on the roles of biblical women. "It's common sense for black people to know their history as it relates to biblical times," says Spann. The women in his classes, he adds, "recognize that biblical women are neglected in Bible study. Whenever I stop to discuss women, a lot of energy is generated in the room."

St. Luke's nerve center for the DISCIPLE program is a narrow office in the church complex; here amid shelves lined with study manuals and boxes of videotapes, a volunteer coordinator and an administrative assistant match facilitators and students to each class. (Registrants are allowed to rank three time preferences and request a particular facilitator, but they are required to take the first in the DISCIPLE series before any of the others.) During the year, the coordinator stays busy marshalling the collective power of the DISCIPLE enrollment.

As students bond to the Word and to one another, the church has found that DISCIPLE classes are primed to take on mission and ministry assignments. In fact, church leadership has ceded specific responsibilities to the student body—taking turns serving meals at a nearby community center, as well as standing with new members when they join, then inviting them to sit in on a class.

In addition, "other ministries in the church contact us when they need power for a cleanup effort in the community or a work team on a neighborhood house," explains DISCIPLE coordinator Barbara Bradford. "We work closely with pastoral care, so we can contact DISCIPLE groups and say, 'This is what needs to be donated to our church food pantry.' Some classes adopt a family for Christmas and continue on with it. Some make it a point to visit in hospitals and jails."

The coordinator also fields requests for DISCIPLE graduates to offer their personal testimonies at other churches trying to start classes. At smaller churches with fewer resources, St. Luke has even sent its own members to lead classes or has underwritten the cost of training members.

DISCIPLE's influence at St. Luke starts at the very top, with its leadership. In the mid-1990s, the church nominating committee mandated that no one could hold an officer's position without completing a long-term Bible study. "We didn't say 'only DISCIPLE,' but the majority of our leaders have taken DISCIPLE," says Holmes. With the underpinnings of a Bible study, he explains, officers "see their leadership position as a ministry. . . . Otherwise, they were seeing it as an ego trip. They would take the leadership position because it was a title, but then they wouldn't follow through, or they'd drop out. We found the people who went through DISCIPLE and really stayed with their groups were our best leaders."

DISCIPLE's lessons of Christian responsibility have also broadened the leadership of St. Luke. "It used to be the few, the faithful who literally ran the church," says Cynthia Ratcliff, whose family joined the church in 1984. "Now everybody literally feels, 'I can take my rightful place; I can lend the gifts I have.' "

Because of the impact of the Bible study, petty squabbling no longer lays claim to church meetings; instead they are perceived as "an opportunity to worship," says Arthur Gregg. Committees sit in a circle and place a lit candle at the center to represent the presence of God. Meetings open with Scripture reading and prayer, and they close with prayer. "We still take care of business, but it's done in a Christian way," says Gregg, the vice-chair of the church council.

The Bible study has worked in other ways. Many say the classes have cultivated a sense of closeness that might otherwise be missing in a church the size of St. Luke. For teenagers, youth DISCIPLE has offered a focus and direction after confirmation classes end. And in each individual class, the fellowship, the peer support, and the spiritual nourishment have proved time and again to strengthen relationships and heal lives. As a result, DISCIPLE has replaced the need for church "care" groups, and the pastoral staff is called upon far less often for counseling.

A Church's Pride, a Pastor's Humility

When Holmes recounts the benefits of DISCIPLE, he keeps returning to the concept of self-identity, of the "cross-shaped church." As he prepared for his retirement in 2002, that sense of church identity took on added meaning. Of course, over the years, he was hardly oblivious to the fact that people were drawn to the church by his powerful presence. But regardless of why they came, they stayed "because they have been connected with the Word," he says. "They understand that they are the church. They can carry on regardless of who's pastor. I think that's very significant."

Yet there's no underestimating church members' love for their former pastor or their pride in his contributions to the DISCIPLE Bible study. Parishioners speak reverently of Holmes's ministry—of his many quiet acts of intercession, of compassion, of consolation. But his preaching (which he continues to do around the country) speaks for itself. With the gift of his voice, he delivers not so much sermons as symphonies, filled with syncopated repetitions, suspense-laden pauses, muted murmurs, and stirring rumbles. "He's got style, but he's not all style," says Harry Wright. "Zan is very intense about the substance, about keeping it real."

Holmes is so much more than that image on the video, those close to him say—and yet that image also reveals him "as the warm, loving, learned man that he truly is," says Martin McLee. "His faith is on his sleeve; his passion for God's people is on his sleeve."

The passion is returned over and over again by the people who have taken DISCIPLE. If there was ever a time Holmes truly felt the impact he's made through the videos, it was in 1999, when his wife of forty-three years died suddenly from a heart attack. As Holmes grieved, he was surprised to receive a flood of condolences from people he'd never met. They were from DISCIPLE participants from all over the country; some cards and letters were signed by entire classes. "Somehow," he says, "the word got out that my wife had died, and you talk about a warm feeling. . . . Words of comfort came from all over the place. They were part of my congregation, my family. That's when I really felt that I was surrounded by friends."

And if there was ever a time when Holmes felt the impact

of DISCIPLE on his own congregation, it came in 1998 during the funeral of a member named S.W. Waiters. Holmes had known Waiters since he was a teenager attending church at the pastor's first appointment. Holmes remembers him as a bright, gregarious young man, a leader, but headed in the wrong direction. He spent much of his early adulthood in prison for armed robbery, and Holmes visited him many times there. Once Waiters was released, he managed to put his life together. He found a job, married, raised a family, and became a devoted member of St. Luke. "He took DISCIPLE 1, 2, and 3, and taught a couple of times," Holmes says. In the mid-1990s, Waiters battled kidney disease, and eventually he succumbed to it. Holmes was there to officiate at the service.

"I went around and viewed his body," the pastor recalls, "and his wife—on his lapel—had put his three DISCIPLE pins—one, two, three. Now, that says it. I get choked up even now when I think about."

CHAPTER EIGHT

A GROWING MINISTRY

I f you don't believe God is full of surprises, then just ask Jim Chaplain, who grew up hating the church and everything it stood for. Or Robert Ward, who had the rare opportunity of imitating Peter one evening and denying three times—to three people—that he was going to be a minister. Or Londia Granger Wright, whose much-loved pastor set her straight as a child by telling her God didn't want girls in the ministry, only boys.

If God isn't full of surprises, then why are all three of these people now preaching the Word?

The call to ordained ministry is, perhaps, one of the most mysterious and awesome aspects of Christian life. Unlike other vocations, it often has nothing to do with the subjects' preferences or inclinations—or even where others have encouraged them to work. But then, didn't God also call an elderly, childless couple named Abraham and Sarah to start a whole nation of people, and a bitter, vengeful tentmaker named Paul to spread the gospel? God has always been full of surprises.

Those who get the call to ministry today often describe it in vividly visceral terms. It's a tug or a pull, insistent and unyielding. It's a push, even a kick, frequently ignored and unwanted. Ultimately, it's a yearning that nothing else can satisfy, a hole that can be filled only by God.

The journeys to full-time ministry are as varied as the people who take them, but Chaplain, Ward, Granger, and an untold number of others all have shared one stop along the way—DISCIPLE Bible study.

The study was created to transform its participants, yet no one could have predicted it would play such a major role in guiding people toward ordained ministry. In fact, admissions officials at several United Methodist seminaries cite DISCIPLE as a common factor in applicants' calls to ministry; some say it's brought up by name by 15 percent or more of those making inquiries. "I've had a recognizably growing number of people mention it over my ten years here," says Chip Aldridge, director of admissions at Wesley Theological Seminary in Washington, D.C. At United Theological Seminary in Dayton, Ohio, director of admissions Doris Whitaker sees why it can make a difference. "It really requires active participation," she says. "They've got to really grapple with the Scripture, and not just let it flow over them like it does on Sunday morning. Unless we're struggling with the Scripture, it doesn't become real."

Three Denials, One Affirmation

For Robert Ward, "real" doesn't begin to describe what he experienced in 1991. When Ward—the manager of an Atlanta recreation center at the time—began to encounter the Bible in his first DISCIPLE class, he felt as if he had been dropped into a Technicolor movie. "I would find myself sitting on the ground," he says, recalling the story of Jesus' feeding of the masses, "and I could look around at the expressions of the people, and I would know, there's a kid out there with fishes and bread." Every other reading, he says, was just as spellbinding. "I was drawn in as one of those people, even with those who were cheering and crucifying Jesus. I was there!"

Growing up poor in Savannah, Ward attended a neighborhood Presbyterian church on his own; he walked down the aisle by himself to join when he was twelve years old. "I just knew," he says, "that's what I was supposed to do, and where I was supposed to be." Ward looks back on those years as the time when he came to believe in God, and yet, he knows now, he had no real grasp of his relationship with God.

After college, he married, moved to Atlanta, and started working at city recreation centers. "It was a most rewarding career," he says. Eventually, the Wards had two sons and they found a church home at Central United Methodist, but they did little more than attend service on Sundays—and sometimes not even that. Then in 1991 the new pastor invited both Ward and his wife to join a DISCIPLE class. "I was worried about the class—thirty-four weeks? . . . But I thought, this is going to be fun. It's going to be good, and I said to my wife, 'Let's take it together.' "

Though Ward had read parts of the Bible before, this was his first introduction to the whole sweep of Scripture, and it began to move him in profound ways. For the first time, he says, "I came to know God as everything I need, everything there is, everything we hope to experience." He also came to understand that he belonged to God. Now, he wondered, what was he going to do about it?

During the course of the study, Ward recalls how unsettled he felt when he read the story of Peter's denials the night before Jesus' crucifixion. He couldn't help but revisit an evening spent with old friends years before in Savannah. During the get-together, one friend came up and said, "I hear you're going to be a preacher." Ward laughed and told him he'd heard wrong. A half-hour later, another friend approached with the same comment. Again, Ward refuted it. And still later, yet another friend asked, Was he going to be a preacher? Once more, Ward said no.

Now, climbing inside Peter's heart as he read the Gospel, Ward suddenly felt burdened by his own denials—denials that he'd previously brushed off so quickly. But still, a preacher? How could he possibly qualify for what he considered "God's highest calling"?

Ward went on to take DISCIPLE: INTO THE WORD INTO THE WORLD; then he and his wife led two youth classes of DISCIPLE. In 1996 he was leading a prayer-and-praise class when a longtime church member dropped in to visit. Afterward, she cornered him. "Robert," she said, "I think you need to attend seminary." It was a comment he knew he couldn't take lightly. She was, after all, the registrar at a local seminary.

From then on, the idea gnawed at him. Finally, he confided his longings to enter seminary to his wife. "I knew it," she said. "God told me you would be going." Remembering the scene, Ward laughs. "I said, 'Why didn't you tell me?'"

Over the next three years, Ward managed to complete seminary while still holding down his job. "I didn't have to borrow a dime," he says. "It just happened. The money was just there." At age forty-eight, he began his full-time ministry, and today he pastors a 300-member church in Covington, Georgia.

"I get a kick out of it every day," he says. "There's a joy I really can't explain. I'm always thinking about God; I'm constantly wanting to know where God is moving and where I fit in. I love to see people receive God and understand the relationship God has with them. Those days you live for. That's really what life is all about."

Overwhelmed by Longing

Londia Granger Wright spent most of her life fighting her call to the ministry. A St. Louis native, she was taught, at an early age, that's what she was supposed to do. Her first lesson came at age eight from her Pentecostal pastor, after Wright announced she wanted to preach like him when she grew up. "He sat me on his knee and hugged me and said I was sweet and sensitive," she recalls, "and then he said I was mistaken. He told me God did not call little girls to the ministry; God only called little boys. I cried, and he hugged me. It hurt very much, but I had such respect for him and I believed what he said. So I did accept it."

By the time she reached adulthood, she had left the Pentecostal church, but still the door to her dream remained shut. She had married a seminary student, who let her know that one minister in the family was enough. Wright contented herself with volunteer church work and a successful career in public relations, mostly for school districts. "I was very involved in the church and I enjoyed it," she says. "But I always wondered what it would be like to be a pastor."

After fourteen years, the marriage collapsed and two years later Wright began dating a man from Kansas City, Missouri. Once she realized the relationship was turning serious, she brought up the crucial question: How would he feel about being married to a minister? "He said, if God called me, then I should heed it," Wright remembers. "That was the first time I'd ever heard anyone say that to me."

But even after Wright had remarried and relocated to Kansas City, she still felt it was better to keep to familiar ways. She took a well-paying job as the public relations officer for the City of St. Joseph, Missouri, and she did volunteer work at her United Methodist church. During service one Sunday, the DISCIPLE coordinator announced a new Bible study class was forming. Wright's interest was piqued when she heard it was for thirty-four weeks. "I thought, that's what I need," she says. "I thought something that substantial will probably satisfy the longing."

Instead, the discipline of the daily reading and weekly classes only intensified her longing. When God asked, in Isaiah 6:8, "Whom shall I send? And who will go for us?" (NIV), Wright felt as if she herself was being questioned. And in Luke 18, when Jesus told the ruler that it wasn't enough to keep the commandments—that he also had to renounce his wealth and follow Christ—Wright felt the demand being placed on her.

After completing the first DISCIPLE study, she started over again, this time as the class leader. As the weeks went by, she says, the longing became "overwhelming." In church on Sunday, she felt as if she were being pushed out of her seat during the sermons. "It was an overpowering sense that I wasn't supposed to be sitting," Wright says. As she watched her pastor administer communion, tears trickled down her cheeks—placed there, she knew, because "I was supposed to be doing it."

She confessed her experiences to her associate pastor. He laughed sympathetically. "You've got it bad," he declared. It was the final nudge she needed. At first, she enrolled in a few classes at St. Paul School of Theology in Kansas City while she kept working. But at the end of 2000, at age forty-five, she made the break complete. She quit her job and enrolled full-time in seminary.

One of the most joyful moments in her journey came when she announced to her DISCIPLE classmates that she was going to pursue ordained ministry; shouts went up, then tears and embraces followed. "That's one of the beauties of DISCIPLE, of course," Wright says. "You receive that confirmation."

Where Is God Calling Me?

The seminary students influenced by DISCIPLE tend to be at least in their thirties and forties, admissions officials say; they've often forsaken successful careers to answer their calls. For the younger seminarians, an episode at a camp, revival, or retreat is more likely to be the time of personal revelation. So it was for Kevin Pees, who was a student at Ohio State University when he had what he calls a "mountaintop experience" during a Christian retreat. DISCIPLE wouldn't come until later. But when it did, the Bible study delivered something just as essential—spiritual depth.

A lifelong Methodist, Pees eagerly became involved in the campus ministry after he enrolled in 1988. But his sights were set on agricultural engineering, and he believed that God was approving his decision. During his junior year, while on a weekend retreat at a camp in the country, Pees found a quiet place to pray; he always tried to listen for a response from God, but never had it come so distinctly. From out of nowhere, he heard a voice say, "Give up engineering."

"It was that brief," says Pees. "No details." He laughs. Even now he's astonished it happened. "There I was, three-quarters finished with college, and I thought, this has to be crazy! I don't think I can do this. No way! Of course, it's foolish to think that God is speaking to you and you're saying, 'No way.' You look back and think, how dense am I?" He laughs again. "But as I sat there, a sense of peace came over me, . . . and I knew I may not go back that week and change my major, but I needed to be prepared for a time when I would give up engineering."

His excitement over this brief moment carried him through that spring and summer. But by fall, he admits, he began to feel unsettled; in two semesters he'd have an engineering degree, and he was no further along in discerning his call. At the same time, the Methodist campus ministry was starting a DISCIPLE class. Pees decided to enroll.

Though he'd read the Bible before, he'd never had an experience like this. "Because we had the common ground of the study, there was a unity that allowed us to deepen our conversation," he says.

Each night, no matter how late he'd stayed up with his engineering textbooks, he always ended the evening with the Bible. "It was kind of like laying my head on a rock. . . . I think of Jacob. He used a rock for a pillow. In a sense, it was concluding my day on a foundation."

Writing in his study manual, Pees wrestled with discerning the shape and direction of his calling. In a lesson on Moses, for instance, he wrote, "How do I try to slough off God's call?" and "Where is God calling me that maybe I'm not hearing or listening?"

By the time he reached Lesson 33—the discernment of gifts—he felt he had his answer. "I recognized that one of the gifts that God was giving me was the 'gift of being an apostle,' which is defined in this setting as a person who would be in full-time ministry—basically, a pastor." His classmates eagerly affirmed him, lifting up his gifts of "administration," "teaching," "compassion," and "prayer." The study posed the question, "How can you act on that call?" Pees wrote, "Be patient and strive to grow in the Spirit." He says now, "I recognized that this was a call to the ministry, but I hadn't been given my marching orders."

He finally got them, less than three years later. After he graduated from college, he went to work in his field; but he meticulously tucked away every extra penny in preparation for seminary. In 1994 he and his wife moved to Kentucky, where he entered Asbury Theological Seminary. Today, he pastors two churches in rural Ohio near where he grew up.

As he looks back, he relies on Jesus' parable of the scattered seeds to describe what the Bible study meant to him. "It kept me from the rocky soil," he says. "It allowed the gospel to take root and grow deeply."

Out of Tragedy Faith Grows

Kevin Pees's moment of reckoning was foreseeable; he knew there was a decision to be made, and he had time to plan and prepare. But there are other life-changing moments that arrive unexpectedly, shattering everyday certainties with the force of a sledgehammer. "Your sister is dying of cancer." "Your daughter has been killed in a car accident." Now what?

For Mike Cave, who lost his younger sister to Hodgkin's disease, it was a time to discover new meaning in his faith. Why, he wanted to know, had God let this happen? For Beryl Notman, whose daughter was killed a few months before high school graduation, it was a time to look for new meaning in her life. How, she wanted to know, did God expect her to pick up the pieces and go on? Their search for answers led both Cave and Notman into DISCIPLE Bible study.

In 1986 Cave was a successful advertising executive in San Antonio who worked hard five days a week, set aside Saturday to "party, party, party," then went to church on Sunday. His life fit into tidy compartments, and he moved along straight, well-marked lines. Then, at age thirty-seven, he learned his twenty-one-year-old sister, Carol—his adored little sister, a college student at the University of Texas at Austin—had been diagnosed with lymphoma. After a year of treatment, she was fighting for her life. In the summer of 1987, Cave took turns with his wife and other members of his family staying at the hospital; in spare moments, he scoured self-help books, frantically trying to make sense of his sister's suffering. One night, at home by himself, "I opened the refrigerator door, found a bottle of wine, and drank the whole thing. I stood in the middle of the living room, just screaming at God about why this was happening. I looked at myself, and thought, God, why don't you take me? If you have to take someone, why not the greater of the two sinners?"

Two years before, Cave had been picked up for drinking and driving, and he'd spent a night in jail. At the time, he'd chalked up the experience as a brief, unfortunate episode; but now it had become hard evidence that God was punishing the wrong person. "I had concocted some terrible theology about how God dispenses mercy," he says. "It's an understanding that . . . if you do the right things, God will reward you. It's a completely graceless way of living."

Carol Cave died in August 1987, and over the next year Cave's guilt and fruitless search for answers continued. Then something happened; call it a small sign. One day, after Cave had stopped by the church to drop something off, he discovered he'd locked his keys in the car. Once he walked back into church and had to sheepishly admit to Tom McClung what he'd done, his pastor smiled and said, "I think God wants you to talk." Sitting in McClung's office, Cave spoke about how he was struggling to read the Bible.

"What are you doing?" the pastor asked.

"I've started with Genesis," Cave answered, "and I'm going to work my way through."

McClung laughed. "Don't do that," he said. "You're going to get to Leviticus, think that's the worst book you've ever read, and put it down forever!"

Then the pastor invited him to join a DISCIPLE Bible study he was about to start. Cave knew instantly he wanted to do it. He and his wife both ended up enrolling in the class.

Once he began DISCIPLE, Cave felt himself, lesson by lesson, being drawn deeper into the Word. "I began looking at my own understanding of faith and realizing there was something flawed, but I couldn't figure it out," he says. As he poured over the Gospels, he could sense a fog was lifting. Meditating on Christ's death and resurrection, he felt for the first time at peace with his sister's death. "That was when I learned that I didn't have to have the answers. I knew I had to learn to live with the uncertainty that life brings."

Why Carol? Ultimately, Cave decided, "Why not Carol? That sounds silly, but that may be the answer. Disease is part of the brokenness of our imperfect world, but it is not something that God gives."

Finally, Cave figured, he'd gotten what he'd been searching for—but he was in for a shock when the class met for Lesson 33. One by one, the students identified the gifts they saw in one another. Cave's turn in the hot seat was last, and McClung had the final word.

"You know," he said, "you really ought to consider being a minister.'"

Cave was speechless. He thought McClung was crazy. Driving home with his wife, Cave was still laughing about it. Then he realized why he was laughing. "I knew he was right—that's it. That's what's missing. That's the hole in my life, the one we stuff with other things—alcohol, work, everything else. That's the hole that only God can fill. I couldn't believe it."

After a year and a half of struggling with the call, he finished out his advertising career and entered Perkins School of Theology in Dallas. Today he is the pastor of a 750-member United Methodist church in Universal City, Texas. "When Tom said what he did, I needed it," he says. "I needed to hear it openly, so I could begin wrestling with it. And I couldn't have begun, if not for the thirty-something weeks that had come before."

For Beryl Notman, the abruptness of tragedy was breathtaking. One Friday evening she had an ordinary family dinner with her seventeen-year-old daughter, Andrea; a few hours later, a voice at the other end of her telephone line was saying Andrea was dead. The girl had caught a ride at a party; the car skidded into a tree just two blocks from the Notman family's home in Enfield, Connecticut. The other three teenagers in the sedan walked away from the accident. Now Notman and her husband were faced with burying the youngest of their three children—a "movie-star-beautiful girl, a neat kid," as her Methodist pastor, Charles Whitford, describes her.

Whitford was the one who suggested to Notman that she train to lead DISCIPLE Bible study. He extended the invitation only about a month after Andrea's death in October 1990, because "I thought it would help her continue a journey that she had begun, and it would give her a community," he says. Notman, an insurance-contract analyst at the time, had always been active in church, and she was now finding some solace in her faith. "I'd do things like take the Methodist hymnal to the cemetery and read the words of the hymns over and over again—'Amazing Grace,' 'A Mighty Fortress Is Our God,' any of them," she says. Notman's battle was less with God than with her sense of hopelessness. How could she go on, she wondered, without her daughter? The loss made her feel isolated, yet instinctively she also knew she needed to be with people. She agreed to go with Whitford to the training the next March.

Once at the training seminar, she found a place at one of the large tables and introduced herself to the woman sitting next to her. They begin to chat; and when Notman told her about Andrea, the woman revealed that she too had lost a child. Her daughter had been murdered. "And I thought, oh my word, that's even worse than my daughter," Notman says. In a split second, her entire perspective changed; of course she wasn't alone in her suffering.

That next fall, less than a year after Andrea's death, she began co-leading a DISCIPLE class. "It really was my lifeline," she says. "If it hadn't been there, I would have just drifted." Scripture seemed to continually speak to her grief; she filled her study manual with references to her daughter, as well as to her own struggle to find purpose.

In the spring of 1992, as the class was in its final weeks, Notman made another visit to the cemetery. This time, the mother of the boy who drove the car also was at Andrea's grave. The two had talked before; Notman greeted her.

"I don't see how you cope with this," the woman said.

"I don't have a choice," Notman replied.

The woman left soon afterward, and Notman began to meditate. Within moments, she knew she was wrong. She did have a choice. "It came to me: 'Choose life.' I remember we had that in DISCIPLE in Deuteronomy (30:19)." Life, she recognized, is both short and precious, and God was calling her to use hers in new ways. Though she didn't know what path she would take, "I was going to do something to try to make a difference in the world."

A couple of months later, she attended an ordination consecration service, "and the bishop invited people to come forward if they were thinking of the ministry, and I was sitting there and I thought, 'Does that mean me?' I felt that I needed to go forward, . . . but I didn't." The next day, at the Sunday service, she got a second chance, and she made her way down the aisle. After a year of discernment, she started her seminary studies at age fifty-three. Today, she pastors a small United Methodist church in Ludlow, Massachusetts.

Even in the midst of her grief, Notman knows, God was leading her to a new purpose. "No one knows if they have tomorrow—that's very real to me," she says. "So why not take more risks? Why not listen to what God is saying?"

Cracking the Exterior, Filling the Void

Perhaps no journey to the ministry is longer than the one that begins with rejecting the church. This was where Jim Chaplain began—as a boy, listening to a preacher in Weiner, Arkansas, who "taught me a whole lot about going to hell but not a lot about grace." Every week he heard about a God who seemed to be "some angry old wizard sitting back looking for an excuse to zap you." Chaplain knew he couldn't keep himself from straying, "so I figured, if you trip up and end up burning in hell, why bother? Just go on and have fun."

As a young man, he lived hard and fast, knocking around

on the drag-racing circuit as a car mechanic. When he finally settled down in Jonesboro, Arkansas, he jumped from one career to the next—setting up television satellite dishes, configuring computer networks, customizing diesel engines. He had a knack for working with electronics, but he also was restless. "I'd done all these things, but there was always a void," he says. "I guess I'd come to believe that's just the way things are."

In 1994, when he was thirty-seven, Chaplain grudgingly found himself back in church, but only as a favor to his mother. She'd had a stroke and needed someone to take her. By now, she'd switched to a United Methodist congregation, but it made little difference to Chaplain. The only reason he was sitting in a pew was so his mother would have a ride home. Of course, he couldn't help but hear the sermons, and he couldn't help but notice there was no longer a whole lot of talk about hell. "After a time," he says, "it got to the point I wasn't so much going for my mother as I was going for me."

Tommy Toombs, pastor of the church, remembers when he first got to know Chaplain. "I saw a man who was bitter, who had a violent temper, who had no use for the church or anything that related to God," he says. "He'd cuss and throw things if things didn't work just right." Toombs, though, could also see that the anger was the hardened exterior of a deeply unhappy man. Underneath, he sensed, "Jimmy had a good heart."

For Christmas one year, Toombs presented Chaplain with a Bible. "Man," Chaplain said, "why don't you spend some money on someone who will read it?" But Toombs insisted; he opened the book and showed how he'd already written Chaplain's name in it. "And anyway," the pastor said, "you'll read it."

"Well, he was right," says Chaplain. "I just picked it up, and I began to read. And I'm kind of a nutty person; if I decide to do something, I do it 100 percent. So once I started, I read a great deal."

Toombs noticed a crack in the exterior. He had an idea: He wanted to bring DISCIPLE to his church, but he needed a scout; he asked Chaplain to enroll in the Bible study at a nearby church. By now, Chaplain trusted his pastor; he agreed to go. Within weeks, Toombs regretted his idea. The group wasn't being led according to the prescribed approach; instead of facilitating a discussion, the leader was lecturing.

"I'm not sure the person had been trained," says Toombs. "Jim would call me every night, saying, 'Tommy, this is awful. I hate it. This is awful.' I said, 'Jim, something's wrong, son.' I had to beg him—beg him—to go to Little Rock to be trained as a leader. And let me tell you what happened: In the three days of training, he came back transformed. I mean, he came back a different person. He saw what DISCIPLE really was meant to do."

After twenty-four people—including Toombs—signed up to take the Bible study, Chaplain wound up leading two classes. He was, says Toombs, "as good a DISCIPLE teacher as you'd ever want." But the pastor saw even more potential. "I could see the way his theology changed, that he knew God wasn't mad at him, that God was merciful and full of grace," Toombs says. "You could sense that God had something more for him to do."

But whenever Toombs brought up a possible call to the ministry, Chaplain had a stock response: "Aw, shut up." Toombs wouldn't let go. He coaxed Chaplain into seeking certification as a lay speaker, just to get a feel for the pulpit. A year later, Chaplain found himself before a board of ministers, explaining why he felt the call to be ordained. "Look," he told the panel, "you folks may have seen a burning bush, but I sure didn't. For me, it just seemed like I was searching for peace, and this was the only place I could find it. I guess it's possible to say no, but for me, I couldn't be at peace and say no."

Chaplain now pastors two small churches in northeast Arkansas while he attends seminary in Memphis. He's found his peace, he says, and he found it through Bible study. "I know people in the ministry who have never taken DISCIPLE," he says, "but for me, I don't know that it would have happened."

Yes, he says, a number of people have pointed out he has a career to match his name. "I just tell them that, for anybody who knew me, it hasn't always been that way."

CHAPTER NINE

YOUNG VOICES

Karl Barth, the eminent twentieth-century theologian, wrote literally millions of words about the Bible, yet when a reporter once asked him to summarize all of Scripture, his answer was succinct: "Jesus loves me."

His response exposes a certain symmetry in Christian theology: What are probably the first words taught to a child in church can also be considered the last words on the subject. But coming full circle—from that rote repetition of a children's song to a profound realization of God's transcendent love—is a journey paved with mystery and complexity. Bible studies can help seekers figure out how to make their way through God's Word. But just as important as *how* is *when*.

At what age can young people move past the simple songs and storybook lessons of Sunday school and plunge into the heart of the Bible?

Cheryl Rude pinpoints that moment in adolescence when "you are just starting to ask the really deep questions . . .

What am I going to do with my life? How do I know if it's the right thing to do? How do I know when God is speaking to me?"

Rude led what is quite possibly the first DISCIPLE class specifically for young people. In 1987 she was the youth director at First United Methodist Church in Wichita, Kansas, the former church of Bible study coauthor Richard Wilke. Soon after DISCIPLE debuted, she personally tailored it for a group of teenagers. Two years later, while serving as a youth director at Highland Park United Methodist Church in Dallas, she and codirector Susan Fuquay were chosen to edit the youth edition of the Bible study.

Over the years, Rude has led both adult and youth groups in DISCIPLE, and she has noticed time and again how differently the younger ages encounter the Bible. No wonder: Adolescence and young adulthood are stages of life utterly unlike any other. They are years filled with unprecedented confusion, pressure, and choices, all arriving at a helter-skelter pace. A Bible study can offer young people not only a stabilizer but also a turning point.

"I'd say it's much more pivotal for youth," says Rude, who went on to become director of leadership development at Southwestern College in Winfield, Kansas. "It comes at a part of your life when you're shaping your identity."

Among Rude's most memorable participants was a girl in that first DISCIPLE class. Carolyn Edwards was a well-liked leader in the church youth group, and Rude made it a point to personally invite her to take the Bible study. But after one of the early sessions, the teen came to Rude and told her she was disappointed. She had thought the study would be more like the free-wheeling discussions of church youth get-togethers.

"All we do," she complained, "is talk about the Bible."

Rude didn't budge. "If you're going to be in this," she replied, "that's what we're going to be doing, so you need to decide."

The next week, the teen returned, and she kept coming back. At the study's close, Rude recalls, "She stood up and said, 'I am so thankful I've been in this group. I'm leaving to go to college, and I'm not going alone. If I hadn't taken DISCIPLE, I wouldn't have understood that I would be taking Jesus as my own personal Savior.' "

Today, Carolyn—now Carolyn Edwards Douglass—makes her career in youth ministry and Christian education in Birmingham, Alabama. She looks upon that DISCIPLE class as the time when her faith blossomed. It also gave her the opportunity, she says, to wrestle with issues that had been weighing heavily on her. Before she became involved in the church youth group, she'd gone through what she calls a "wild child" phase of underage drinking. In DISCIPLE she was able to deal with her guilt and put the experience in perspective.

"I started reading about these people who messed up all the time, but God still loved them. God said bring all your baggage and come with me," says Douglass. "I learned that the purpose of Christianity isn't to be good. The purpose is to have this relationship with God, and—by the way—that can help you make better choices. Sin is something that separates us from God. It's something that separates us from the life he wants us to lead—a more whole, abundant life."

Sharing the Struggles

DISCIPLE isn't necessarily an experience every teenager is ready for, say adults who have led classes. The reading assignments and structured discussions are demanding, especially when shoehorned into schedules already packed with classes, homework, and extracurricular activities.

Tammy Lane, a student minister at Third Baptist Church in Chicago, has found that a certain type of teen—bright, outgoing, and self-motivated—gravitates toward DISCIPLE. In her classes, they also have all happened to be girls.

"They've wanted to strengthen their faith," says Lane, "and to get help standing up to peer pressure and all the other things high school brings their way. They're worried about fitting in, which I guess is the normal thing, but they have such high standards they don't want to be part of a crowd that goes in the wrong direction. They're living holy lives, but they have friends who may not be; so they're trying to keep their friends out of trouble. I think they're like the voice of God in the midst of their friends."

At Broadmoor United Methodist Church in Baton Rouge, Louisiana, Jodie Harper noticed that the boys and girls drawn to the youth classes she taught for several years all had a willingness to be vulnerable—far more than the adults she's also led in DISCIPLE. "They shared really personal things—struggles with parents, struggles with friends and spirituality, struggles with temptation," she says. "For instance, what do you do when you're at a party and everybody's drinking and you're a Christian? They've been sexually tempted that way, too. There are a lot of things that teenagers have in their faces all the time."

Experience quickly taught Harper to leave at least half an hour for the group prayer at the close of each lesson. As the teens took turns offering their prayer concerns, tears often flowed. "That's the time when they shared some of their deepest hurts," she says. "A lot of times they had a friend who was suicidal or taking drugs. . . . A lot of times they prayed about safety. At that age, they think they're invincible, but we had a lot of 'my friend's friend was in an accident or in a coma or was killed.' Even though they had a sense of invincibility, they prayed a lot for safety. And they prayed a lot for friends."

Andrew Roberts was a high school junior when he jumped at the chance to take one of Harper's classes in 1998. At the time, he was just emerging from several difficult years. Teased and taunted in middle school for being overweight, he became depressed and developed an eating disorder. His life began to turn around, he says, when he realized he could find strength in God. By his sophomore year, he had felt a call to the ministry, and he attempted to read the Bible on his own. "What I ended up doing was buying some of the inspirational books and looking in the Bible for the passages they cited," he recalls. "But that was more about trying to fill a specific need and not trying to grow in God."

With DISCIPLE, Roberts found the big picture he was hungry for. He also found something he hadn't anticipated—a group of peers he could finally trust. It took him several weeks, he admits, to open up during prayer time. "At first I was sharing 'I have a test tomorrow,' but at the end, I was praying for things in my spiritual life," he says.

Roberts admits he resisted the structure of the readings at first, but as the weeks went by, he began to realize the Bible was working on him in subtle and unexpected ways. It wasn't, as he had previously thought, just a series of ancient stories; it was a world inhabited by people he could relate to.

"The Bible is the story of our lives," he says. "The whole thing is a culmination of what we go through. It made my relationship with God much more personal. . . . We'll never be able to truly understand the love God has for us. But if we stop looking for the understanding, and just feel it, it's something that grows so much in our lives."

Roberts has since continued on with his schooling at Louisiana State University, and he remains committed to answering his call to ordained ministry. "Today, as I try to be who I want to be, I'm not fulfilled," he says. "That's not who I am. Who I am is who God wants me to be, and that's what I strive to be every day. DISCIPLE helped me really discern that and get a real grasp of how that has an interaction in my life."

A Duty Becomes an Awakening

For many of the youth who enroll in DISCIPLE, faith has previously been a matter of emulating parents and grandparents. They've followed their elders to church, listened to their spiritual guidance, absorbed their moral authority. DISCIPLE then offers these young people an opportunity to claim their faith as their own. Sometimes it can prove to be an unsettling experience.

When campus minister Glenn Tyndall led a Bible study for college students at Virginia Tech, one of the young women in class began to cry during the discussion of the first chapters of Genesis. The lesson described how the two Creation stories—the story of God creating the universe in six days and the story of Adam and Eve—evolved separately out of the narrative traditions of two different cultures. The student had believed the stories were successive, and that they should be taken at face value. "She said, 'I understand what you're saying and it makes sense, but this is stuff I picked up from my grandmother, and it's hard to let go,' " Tyndall recalls. "What we tried to tell her is that we weren't tearing down her grandmother. . . . But at some point we all have to accept responsibility for our thinking, rather than be bound by what may have been an uninformed point of view."

Until he took DISCIPLE in 1996 during his senior year in high school, Ed Beaver says he was doing little more than going through the motions in his spiritual development. "I was attending my parents' church, and I was doing my parents' thing," says Beaver, who grew up in Laurel, Maryland. "I went through confirmation in seventh grade, but I think it's almost done for your parents to see you do it. I felt I was way too young to really grasp the concepts."

Even when he signed up for the Bible study at his church in nearby Highland, "it probably felt more like a duty," he says. "It felt like 'that's what a good Christian does.' "

But duty soon turned into what Beaver describes as "an awakening." In revisiting the Bible stories he'd first heard as a child in Sunday school, he was delighted he was no longer getting what he calls the "Mickey Mouse" version. "I was filling in the gaps and the *whys,*" he says. By the time he had completed the Bible study, he looked upon it as his "personal confirmation" of faith.

His group leader, Pete Conner, watched with satisfaction as Beaver and the other students made the transition. "I think that the Bible put a new set of spectacles on them," says Conner, an Ashton, Maryland, business manager whose daughter was also in the class. "I think most of them, when they came, thought they knew right from wrong. But I knew that would be challenged at some point. . . . Of course, you learn from your parents, but when you see the lesson come from a greater authority, it takes on a deeper significance."

Once Beaver enrolled as a history major at the University of Maryland at Baltimore County, he took courses that examined early Judaism, and he also had a serious relationship with a young Catholic woman—two experiences that made him confront his newly ignited faith. For a time, he drifted away from church participation. But since he graduated in 2001, he has returned to the fold, even volunteering with his church youth group. "When you're on your spiritual journey, there are times when you're walking, almost running, and there are times when you're standing still. I feel like now I'm just starting to move again." Without DISCIPLE, he says, "I don't think I would have survived through college having the same faith that I do."

Questions and More Questions

The tide of imponderables that rises in adolescence and young adulthood can come in the midst of pain: Why did my friend have to die? Or in a fog of philosophical befuddlement: If God created everything, then what created God?

The questions can range from mildly perplexing to deeply disturbing, yet those who take DISCIPLE learn they can't escape the questions. "I think if you can't ask questions, then you don't have a foundation," says Amy Emerson, who has taken and co-led DISCIPLE classes at Virginia Tech in Blacksburg. "If you don't have questions, you will never grow."

Emerson studies astrophysics, the science of the universe. "The language of my life is logic," she says, "and it always has been." Growing up in the church, she compartmentalized her religion away from her scientific intellect, believing she would never be able to reconcile the two.

Once at college, though, she found her community of friends at the Methodist campus ministry, and she began dipping into the Scriptures and taking short-term Bible studies. "I got to the point where I was ready to have more," she says, "and there was more for me to have." As she entered graduate school, she enrolled in DISCIPLE and it "just opened the door." Making her way through the lessons, she began to see that her logical mind was not necessarily in conflict with her faith. "That is the way I question my faith," she says, "and it's the way my faith continues to grow. . . . The only thing I give up to faith is the fact that there is a God—there is a supreme being who gave order to chaos—and I can't explain that," she says. "I do believe that when the universe was created, it was created through God. Why? Because it's just so beautiful. It's amazingly old and beautiful. If you can define that without God, you're overestimating something."

When Jenny Mitchell took DISCIPLE as a junior in high school, she also felt herself in the grip of questions. That first Bible study, in 1988, touched off a concerted quest for answers, a quest that lasted nine years and took her through three more DISCIPLE Bible studies.

Mitchell says she has always been "a seeker," but during her high school years in Auburn, Washington, she felt especially lost. She had moved to the town before her sophomore year; never able to find a niche at her new school, she suffered through three years of isolation. She also endured the back-to-back loss of her maternal grandparents, and their deaths touched off conflicts in her mother's family that left the teenager angry and confused.

The Sunday school for youth at her church, Auburn First United Methodist, offered her few insights. "We'd talk about the parables and whatever was in the lesson plan," she recalls, "but we never talked about how it applied to your life."

When her pastor, Bob Ward, invited Mitchell to join the adult Bible study he was forming, she accepted without hesitation. "I knew it was going to be a lot of reading," she says, "and I thought, 'So what? It's like I'm taking another class.' "

Making her way through the Bible that year, Mitchell enjoyed being able to grasp the common themes. She also gained an important new perspective from her adult classmates. As she listened to their individual anguishes—over family illness, a spouse's death, the breakup of a marriage— she realized how much struggle is just a part of life. "I think I got out of the teenage perspective of everything being about me," she says.

Something else in the class caught her attention as well: Questions were being asked, but not necessarily answered. Ward, who co-led the class, often would bring discussions to a close simply by saying, "Let's move on." One night, during a lesson on the Holy Spirit, the other co-leader confessed, "I have no answers. I just have a lot of questions." Mitchell was bewildered by the comment. "It was the first time," she says, "I saw someone in an adult leader role stop and say, 'I don't have all the answers.' "

But answers were still what Mitchell wanted. When the

Bible study was completed, she still felt an emptiness.

Once in college, she took DISCIPLE: INTO THE WORD INTO THE WORLD twice, and she became involved in a Presbyterian campus fellowship. During those years, she was still trying to make sense of God and the world; but she also was beginning to realize the power of prayer. And she was able to see how her faith wasn't ever going to come in a crashing wave. "It was this trickle," she says, "and it kept happening and happening and happening, and I started to feel it more and realize it more."

By 1997 Mitchell was a twenty-five-year-old schoolteacher in Longview, Washington, when she decided to take the Bible study once again. This time, she co-led a DISCIPLE class with the pastor's wife, Abby Henry, at their church, Kelso First United Methodist.

For the second lesson, Henry had copied onto a poster-size paper a quotation from Ranier Maria Rilke's *Letters to a Young Poet*, and she tacked it up for the class to read:

> Have patience with everything unresolved in your heart and . . . try to love the questions themselves. . . . Don't search for the answers, which could not be given to you now, because you would not be able to live them. And the point is, to live everything. Live the questions now. Perhaps then, someday far in the future, you will gradually, without even noticing it, live your way into the answer.

As Mitchell absorbed the words, she began to see, for the first time, how misguided her search for answers had been. The point, she realized, wasn't so much to find answers as it was to "live the questions."

How could she truly understand God? How could she make sense of all that God had created? The tension in those questions now slipped away. "I know the answer is, God is more than anything I can comprehend," she says. "Not everything needs to be on an intellectual level. God is not just in our brains. Therefore, it's not just my brain that has to understand God. So I just let it be, and I have a calmness and a peace and an awesome reverence."

The spiritual quest of a teenager has long since faded into the past. Now, as an adult, Mitchell has new priorities as she encounters the Bible. "I just know that I want a deeper relationship with God, and I want a deeper relationship with Jesus. And I want answers," she admits. "But I'll 'live the questions.' "

CHAPTER TEN

NO BOUNDARIES

W hen DISCIPLE Bible study was originally developed, its creators thought they were dreaming big to envision a resource for Protestant congregations around the United States. But perhaps they should have taken a lesson from history—for obviously, over the centuries, human dreams have done little to confine the spread of God's Word.

The annals of early Christianity spill over with stories of doors opening, with accounts of improvisation, happenstance, and revelation that kept taking Jesus' message farther and farther. The apostles first believed their mission was simply to bring other Jews to Christ, but of course, the world now knows how profoundly they underestimated the task. Over the centuries, it became clear that no one "owned" this religion. What it was and what it became grew in countless directions from the hearts and souls of the swelling numbers of the faithful.

In a small sense, the same can be said about the spread of

this present-day Bible study series—a fact that the president of The United Methodist Publishing House recognized by the time the second study, INTO THE WORD INTO THE WORLD, had been introduced.

"When we were into it about five years," recalls Robert Feaster, who retired in 1996, "I would have to say DISCIPLE was no longer a program. It was a movement. It's something that took on a life of its own."

Though the publishing house has marketed DISCIPLE in all fifty states, clearly word of mouth has multiplied the Bible study's impact. Those who take DISCIPLE talk about it to family and friends—and often to people they hardly know. Many go on to take the leader training and recruit their own classes. And a few take it to places that none of the study's creators ever imagined.

Some of the fastest growing and most determined grass-roots efforts to spread DISCIPLE have brought it to two new, improbable frontiers—inside the walls of American prisons and across the borders of almost twenty countries, many non-English-speaking.

No matter where they are, the people who take up these new challenges all share extraordinary grit and imagination about spreading God's Word. That doesn't mean, however, they necessarily started out that way. As with the original disciples, sometimes the most unlikely ones are chosen to do God's work.

Doors Keep Opening

For Darrell Sayles, teaching a Bible study to convicts wasn't even on his radar the night in 1995 that he drove to his DISCIPLE class in Greensboro, North Carolina. Along the way to his church, Sayles listened to a Christian radio program on a prison ministry, and it pricked his interest. During a study break, he mused to his classmates, "Wouldn't it be nice if people in prison could experience DISCIPLE?"

He meant it as a wistful notion, no more than if he had said, "Wouldn't it be nice if we had world peace?" But before he'd hardly finished the last syllable, another member of the class, Darrell Hayden, bit on it, as he puts it now, "like a bass jumping on a June bug."

"That's it!" said Hayden. "That's what we need to do! Let's do it!"

The two Darrells had become fast friends during the course of the Bible study. Sayles, an accountant in his mid-forties, was the Darrell with a little more height and a lot more hair. Hayden, a salesman in his late fifties, was the Darrell with a little more belly and a lot more syrup in his Southern drawl.

Hayden knew Sayles was a man serious about his faith. He didn't know, however, that Sayles wasn't serious at all about taking DISCIPLE into a prison. But Sayles was too embarrassed to say anything. When the two men saw each other the next week, Hayden couldn't wait to ask if his friend had contacted a prison. Sayles reluctantly admitted he hadn't. When Hayden kept pestering him, Sayles knew he'd have to confess—or make some show of effort. Thinking, even hoping, that he'd be rejected, he telephoned an official at one of the nearby prisons. But that telephone call led to another and another, and each time Sayles was encouraged to keep going with his idea. Soon, he was talking to a prison chaplain who invited the two men out for a visit.

"One of the people in our DISCIPLE class made the observation once," says Sayles, "that when the Lord opens a door, you've got to walk through it. And the doors just kept opening for me. I kept waiting for the doors to close so I didn't have to do it, but it didn't work out that way."

A few months later, as he and Hayden sat down for the first time to lead a DISCIPLE Bible study for a dozen inmates at a minimum-security state prison, Sayles knew he'd learned something important: God had a claim on his life, whether he felt it or not. "Every Christian should realize we're not going on our own strength to begin with," says Sayles. "As things kept falling into place, I felt more and more that this is what I was supposed to be doing."

Any lingering doubts were erased that first day he passed through the prison gates. "I felt at home," Sayles says.

Spreading the Word

Whether by chance or intent, hundreds of people in pockets around the country—in North Carolina, Pennsylvania, Arkansas, Georgia, Kansas, and Oklahoma, among other states—have led DISCIPLE studies in prisons over the years. With an estimated United States inmate population of two million, the opportunities for this ministry are bountiful.

Leading a DISCIPLE study in prison, say Hayden, Sayles, and others, is both easier and tougher than leading one on the outside. The hardships of prison life can nurture a strong hunger, even a desperation, for God's promise of hope and healing; students often are highly motivated to do not only their homework but also considerable soul-searching. On the other hand, some inmates gravitate to the study for all the wrong reasons.

Sayles and Hayden learned their share of lessons during their first prison experience. "The inmates run the gamut from the ones who are manipulative to those who are struggling to do the right things," says Sayles. Telling the difference between the different types, though, proved to be a challenge.

Kelvin Smith was an inmate in their first class who quickly earned the trust of the two men. Convicted of second-degree murder after killing a close friend in a drunken brawl in 1991, Smith had accepted Christ into his life by the time the DISCIPLE class was offered. To him DISCIPLE was an answer to a prayer. With his parole coming up, he says,

"I needed to be grounded, rooted in the Lord, and I knew an intense study would help prepare me for when I was getting out."

In his struggle to deal with the crime he'd committed, Smith was able to take comfort in two of the great leaders in the Old Testament—Moses, who killed an Egyptian in a rage; and King David, who masterminded the death of Bathsheba's husband, Uriah. "It was wrong of me to take a life," says Smith. "I had to be punished. God is a god of wrath. But the Bible also says he chastens those he loves. . . . Just like Jesus says, no man is completely out of my hand. Every man can be called back to God. That helped me a lot."

Smith was paroled before he finished the Bible study, so Sayles and Hayden arranged for him to complete it in a class at their Greensboro church. He would be the only African-American—not to mention ex-convict—among the group of middle-class whites. "I prayed about it," says Smith, recalling his initial apprehension, "and God said, 'My people are everywhere.' " His new classmates, he says, confirmed it. "They accepted me as another Christian. That, for me, was totally, totally amazing."

Other outcomes weren't so successful for Sayles and Hayden. They took a chance on another inmate in that original class and spoke on his behalf at a parole hearing. After they had finished their plea for his release, a parole official offered an explicit recitation of the vicious crime the inmate had committed. The man they thought had been convicted of involuntary manslaughter had instead been found guilty of premeditated murder.

"Darrell, we've been had," Hayden told his partner after the hearing. "We let our hearts overrule our minds. This guy was a con artist from the word *go.*"

From that moment on, the two men vowed to stay out of parole hearings. "Look," Sayles says, "these folks have committed crimes, and they're paying the penalty. When the Lord's ready to put them back on the street, he will."

Despite the ups and downs, both men eventually became so moved by their prison experience—and by the inmates' responses—they decided it couldn't end with just one class.

Together with Mark Hicks, the associate pastor at their church, they worked to spread the ministry to other prisons. In 1996 volunteers were recruited to take DISCIPLE into two more prisons. That same year, Sayles, Hayden, and Hicks also persuaded the North Carolina secretary of corrections to write a letter to every state prison superintendent endorsing the study. To develop the program, church officials created a task force that put Sayles, Hayden, and Hicks at the helm. A year later sixteen prisons had DISCIPLE classes. By the end of 2001, more than six hundred inmates in North Carolina were taking the Bible study in one halfway house, one federal prison, and more than fifty of the eighty-four prisons in the state system. Hicks oversees the initiative as the executive director of DISCIPLE Bible Outreach Ministries for the entire state, and Hayden works as a full-time missionary. Sayles continues to do what he loves most—leading a DISCIPLE class in prison.

Eventually ex-convict Kelvin Smith ended up back in prison, but this time it was to co-lead a DISCIPLE class. His example, he says, has moved his classmates. "My witness is just that you can do it," says Smith, who lives and works in Winston-Salem. "I guess they look up to me, but I say, 'Don't focus on what I do. Focus on what God will have you do.' "

Hurdles and Stumbling Blocks

The North Carolina initiative is by far the most sophisticated of the DISCIPLE prison ministries. But other efforts are no less heartfelt or determined.

In Georgia, Diane Parrish lobbied state officials for two-and-a-half years before she received approval in December 2001 to take DISCIPLE into prison. To get in, she had to negotiate her way through a litany of strict regulations.

Though she managed to get the guards' hourly count of inmates waived for the classes, study sessions can last no longer than ninety minutes. She also received an exemption from a rule that keeps inmates from receiving books from any source other than a publisher; the study manuals are delivered to prison chaplains, who then distribute them, along with Bibles for the inmates who don't have their own. The plastic comb bindings on the study manuals have to be removed because they have been deemed potential weapons.

The prison rules have left Parrish unfazed. "I can only do it full throttle," she says, "and not be sidetracked by petty little obstacles that are very fixable." As part of a comprehensive program to minister to inmates and their families, DISCIPLE debuted in 2002 at five Georgia state prisons, and Parrish plans to bring it to more. Like Sayles and Hayden in North Carolina, she knows she's reaching into lives that are desperately in need of God's gifts.

"People in prison are, for the most part, completely hopeless," says Parrish, whose Prison Disciple Ministry is based in Marietta. "They're in there for life, knowing their families have completely turned their backs on them, knowing that they are scarred for life, knowing that they are now victims in their own way because the penal system is not always just and fair."

Navigating the regulations is hardly the only hurdle for DISCIPLE prison ministries. The expense of the program is another, since inmates generally can't pay for the materials. Those who lead prison classes usually have relied on the generosity of congregations. Stan Nixon started leading a prison DISCIPLE class in 1999 with $100 donations from each of the five tiny western Pennsylvania congregations he served. In Oklahoma City, Jim Gayle underwrites the prison classes he's led since 1998 with regular contributions from the 150 or so people who worship with him at their church's early Sunday chapel service.

Yet another stumbling block for DISCIPLE prison ministries is the frequency of transfers among penitentiary populations. Inmates are moved from prison to prison sometimes in a matter of months, and whether or not they've finished a Bible study is hardly taken into consideration. In Pennsylvania some transferred inmates have taken their workbooks with them and finished the study on their own. In Oklahoma Jim Gayle has dealt with transfers into prison by leading DISCIPLE nonstop.

Claudia Lovelace, one of his classmates in 1998, well remembers the emotions the Bible study stirred in her group. She took Gayle's class at one of four Redemption Churches, a United Methodist initiative in Oklahoma that inmates are allowed to attend outside of prison. Lovelace, who served eighteen months for a drunken-driving conviction, began DISCIPLE several weeks before her parole and she continued after her release.

Prison life, says Lovelace, is a gauntlet of suspicion and distrust, but she found a safe haven in her DISCIPLE class. "It gave us an example of how to share God's love with one another," she says. "It gave us a real-life experience—how to bond—and for prisoners, that's a big thing, because we're lying, cheating, manipulative people."

After nearly a lifetime of drug and alcohol abuse, Lovelace found her biblical counterparts in Exodus. "I just felt I was one of the Israelites who was given chance after chance after chance after chance," she says, "and I just wasn't getting it. But God was still by my side."

Once she left prison, she entered an alcoholic treatment program. Eventually, she took a job as a "relapse prevention" officer at Redemption Church and, at age fifty, began to answer a call to the ministry. Before prison, she says, "I knew there was another life. I just didn't know how to get there, because there's an abyss—a thing you have to cross to get to it. DISCIPLE is one of those things that helped me get across."

Planting the Seed

When they talk about success, the ministers and laypeople involved in DISCIPLE prison ministries linger on individual stories, such as Lovelace's, rather than recitations of recidivism rates. Studies of prison ministries show significantly fewer re-arrests among paroled participants than among the general population of parolees, says Mark Hicks, director of the North Carolina ministry. Since his program began in 1999, he has tracked a recidivism rate as low as 5 percent among the DISCIPLE graduates paroled in his state.

In Pennsylvania Stan Nixon prefers to beg off when people ask him to quantify the results of what became his full-time ministry in 2001. They're missing the point, he says. "How many people are changed when they leave church on Sunday?" he asks. The faithful are called "to plant the seed," and only God truly knows when it takes root, says the Glasgow, Pennsylvania, minister.

Still, in random conversations, prison staff have told Nixon they've noticed something different about inmates in his classes. "They [staff members] don't exactly know what it is, but they can see transformation in them," he says. "I think it's the self-discipline—studying God's Word every day and making it a part of their lives, putting in the prayer time."

One prison where Nixon has volunteered is a federal unit plagued by tensions between African-American and Hispanic inmates. The classes he's led have been mostly made up of African-Americans; to reach out to both groups, a class was added for Spanish-speaking inmates.

"The first lesson, we handed out the study manuals and also a Spanish study Bible," recalls Dorie Heckman, a church member who co-led the class. "One of the first questions we asked was, 'When did you get your first Bible?' I had three or four gentlemen holding their Bibles with tears in their eyes saying, 'This is my first Bible.' "

At the end of the study, Nixon's class joined Heckman's for a bilingual covenant service. After a summer break, the leaders returned to the prison to discover that both groups had continued meeting together for fellowship and study in the chapel each week. "They made the decision that their faith and need to study were stronger than any language or cultural differences," Heckman says.

That fall the classes merged for praise songs in English and Spanish before splitting up for study. Their newfound brotherhood didn't stay contained within the chapel walls. "They've carried the same compassion out to share it with other people in their culture who may be deeply involved [in the racial tension]," Heckman says. "The chaplains say the effects are being seen in the cafeteria, in the work stations, in the rooms."

To Nixon, DISCIPLE is about tearing down the walls that imprison all of us—the ignorance and prejudice that isolate people from one another and from God. The second year he taught one prison group, Nixon startled his classmates with a revelation that leveled a wall like a blast from Joshua's trumpets. Before he became a minister, Nixon told the convicts, he had worked for several years as a prison guard.

"I wanted them to understand my journey," he says. The response was overwhelming. "They said, 'We have observed you, and we know you have the heart of Christ to come here, and it's not just a job.'"

Yes, Nixon says, his previous work equipped him with experiences and insight that have helped him relate to convicts. But, he adds, he didn't enter the ministry ever intending to return to prison. He knows now that God had a plan. "He prepares us for things yet to come, even before our own understanding."

Moving Across Borders

DISCIPLE has moved into other countries often with that

same kind of Spirit-led serendipity. Occasionally, something as small as a chance conversation has been enough to spark a new ministry in another part of the world.

Such was the case in 2000 when a chat between two strangers waiting for an elevator in Cleveland, Ohio, became the turning point for DISCIPLE's entry into Russia.

One of the men was Richard Wilke. The place was the United Methodist General Conference, the denomination's top legislative body that meets every four years. Wilke and his wife, Julia, had just left a meeting with Ruediger Minor, the bishop appointed to oversee Methodism in Russia. Minor had asked his American colleague to help find the $50,000 needed to launch a DISCIPLE program in the former Communist country, and Wilke had agreed to do it.

"Afterward, Julia asked me, 'How are you going to get the money?' " Wilke recalls, "and I said, 'I have no idea.' "

Moments later, Wilke was at an elevator when a DISCIPLE graduate nearby recognized him. The man, a United Methodist lay leader named Joe Whittemore, struck up a conversation and the two began to talk. Whittemore told how the Bible study had made such an impact on the churches in his home state of Georgia. Wilke thanked him, then abruptly changed the subject to the promise now weighing on his mind.

Whittemore didn't think twice. His church conference, he said, had recently decided to undertake a major international initiative, but it hadn't settled on a particular project.

"I think the Lord just put us together," he told Wilke.

Within months, more than two hundred churches in the North Georgia Conference had raised the funds needed to translate and print the first study manual in the DISCIPLE series, as well as to bring four Russian Methodists to the United States for training.

Similar stories abound, and they seem indicative of how this Bible study has spread around the globe.

By 1989, The United Methodist Publishing House

decided to translate the first study into Korean and later into Spanish. With the Nashville publisher's modest resources, however, DISCIPLE has had limited success among Korean and Spanish-speaking congregations.

Although The United Methodist Publishing House didn't set out to create a product for use internationally, foreign efforts with significant impact have been initiated either by a Methodist publisher in a particular country or by clergy or laypeople located outside the United States.

The study was brought to Indonesia, for example, by Jakarta businesswoman Maimunah Natasha, who happened across a DISCIPLE display at an international church conference in Brazil. Linda Hernandez, a secretary at the Methodist Publishing House in England, "felt a calling" at the first training event in her country, and she went on to coordinate the program for all of Great Britain. Jim Coy, an Evansville, Indiana, businessman with a long track record in mission work, helped launch the study in Liberia, Sierra Leone, and Jamaica.

DISCIPLE was introduced in Malaysia and Singapore by Lee Lee Castor, a Malaysian pastor who became acquainted with it during a short-term appointment in Chattanooga, Tennessee. The movement in Singapore eventually evolved into the DISCIPLE hub for Southeast Asia, extending the Bible study's reach into Vietnam, Taiwan, Laos, Hong Kong, and China.

When approached by foreign contacts, the Nashville publisher eagerly cooperates. For the Singapore venture, for example, the publisher donated the rights to the material. "They wanted it, and we wanted them to have it," explains former publishing house president Robert Feaster. "We were capable of making decisions like that, even though our job was to keep ourselves in business."

Once an international initiative is begun, the publisher works to keep a hands-on approach to ensure the original intent of the study is followed. Though the translation of the study components and the dubbing or subtitling of videos are undertaken by the organizers in each country, the publisher enlists readers in the United States to review the final products.

Wini Grizzle, the publisher's director of seminars, has traveled to many countries over the years to conduct leader-training events. And as with the Russian effort, representatives from other countries regularly come to the United States so they can learn to train leaders. To keep costs down, study materials are printed in each country rather than shipped from the United States.

Occasionally, cultural differences have to be dealt with as translators work their way through the manuals. An assignment to visit a synagogue, for example, would be pointless in a country with no Jewish population. A suggestion to volunteer for a local immunization program would only perplex participants in a country with a national health service. But for such minor exceptions, the Bible study seems to bring a universal message that transcends any language or cultural barrier.

Anecdotes of DISCIPLE experiences in other countries are remarkably similar to those told in the United States. Participants find new meaning for their lives in the Scriptures. Groups bond over the spirited discussions. Many graduates go on to more active roles in their churches and communities.

A Worldwide Christian Community

What sometimes sets the programs in other countries apart from those in the United States, however, is the voracious desire for what most Americans simply take for granted— the opportunity to study God's Word. Some countries where DISCIPLE has gone have legacies of Christian oppression; in others, Christian expression or access to Christian learning is limited. When the Bible study is introduced, it can evoke astounding responses of appreciation, pride, and tenacity.

In Singapore, for instance, a handful of pastors were expected for the rally to introduce DISCIPLE there; more than three hundred swelled the hall. In Hong Kong, Filipino women—who've left their homeland to find work as domestics—meet for DISCIPLE only after they have changed into more dignified uniforms of white blouses and red skirts. In the Czech Republic, organizers collate the study manuals with the only method available—by hand. In Liberia, during civil war, Pastor Blidi Nimley fled the violence that destroyed his church and took with him only two possessions, his Bible and his DISCIPLE study manual.

In Russia, where the Bible was outlawed during nearly seven decades of Soviet control, the program's coordinators had no problem stirring interest in DISCIPLE. "People want to read the Bible here," says Bishop Ruediger Minor, "but not just to read out of curiosity and to start in the wrong places, but to study it systematically."

During the first training event in Russia, held in the summer of 2002, about forty pastors and laypeople met in a former Communist Party facility outside Moscow to learn how to lead a DISCIPLE group. Among those present were the Wilkes, Joe Whittemore, and his wife.

After playing such a key role in starting the program, the Hartwell, Georgia, man wanted to share in the excitement of the occasion. "It was important for us to be there," he says, "to show them, by our presence, that we were interested and that we wanted to be supportive of what they were doing."

During his visit, Whittemore was moved time and again by the people he met and the stories they told. "They love the Bible," he says. "Some of their ancestors have given their lives for it. For seventy years they kept the faith. In many, many ways they have a much stronger faith than we have, because they've been under such tremendous oppression."

Perhaps the most powerful experience came as the Wilkes and Whittemores entered a tiny church for Sunday morning worship. Whittemore found himself apprehensive about how they would be received—these four citizens of a country that once was a sworn enemy. Their first encounter was with three elderly women standing near the door.

"I wasn't sure what to do," Whittemore says. But the women knew. All three walked over and embraced their visitors.

"I think that's when I realized that this is about Christian community," he says. "When Christians get together, it doesn't make any difference what the past has been. We sang with them; we laughed with them; we worshiped with them; we had communion. Spiritually, it was a confirmation that we all belong to the same community, no matter what the differences are."

The universal appeal of DISCIPLE underscores this same message. As the Bible study continues to step into new frontiers, it is sure to touch and transform lives in ways as yet unseen—bringing more and more people together, drawing them to the power of the Word, moving them out into the world. Spiritual journeys have come to be expected with such a trusted and well-tested means of transportation.

"DISCIPLE is like a little sailboat racing with a gust of wind," Wilke says. "It's moved into areas and dimensions that only God could have taken it to. Everyone involved with it understands that. No one dreamed in the early days of the places it would go or the things it would do. Truly, God is in the movement."